Great Defensive Players of the NFL

Exciting sketches of twelve of pro football's most formidable defensive stars: Sam Huff, Willie Davis, Larry Wilson, Tommy Nobis, Gino Marchetti, Bob Lilly, Joe Schmidt, Dave "Deacon" Jones, Chuck Bednarik, Henry Jordan, Dick "Night Train" Lane, and Dick Butkus.

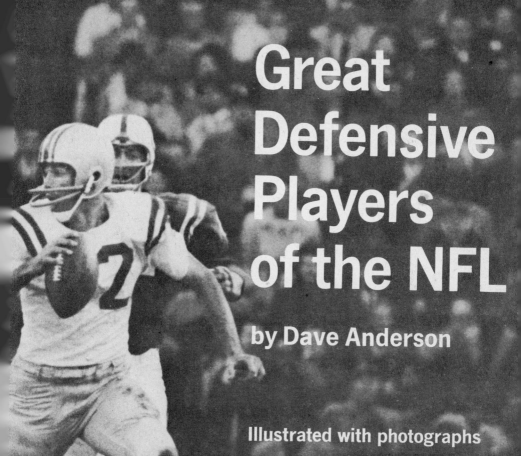

Great
Defensive
Players
of the NFL

by Dave Anderson

Illustrated with photographs

THE PUNT PASS AND KICK LIBRARY
NFL

RANDOM HOUSE
NEW YORK

Photograph credits: Vernon J. Biever, 18, 30, 46, 82, 104, 107, 134, 140, 145, 151, 157, 162, 165; Dallas Cowboys, 76; Malcolm Emmons, 25, 35, 58, 67, 102, 111, 137; Walter Iooss, Jr., ii-iii; The News, 131; Ken Regan, viii, 2, 12, 44, 49, 60, 73, 79, 90, 118, 121, 126-127, 148, 171; T. Tomsic, vi-vii; UPI, 15, 23, 87, 93, 96, 116; Herb Weitman, St. Louis Cardinals, 32; Wide World, 6-7, 39, 55, 70, 160, 174. Cover: Vernon J. Biever

This title was originally cataloged by the Library of Congress as follows:
Anderson, Dave.
Great defensive players of the NFL. New York, Random House [1967]
x, 176 p. ports. 22 cm. (The Punt, pass, and kick library 7)
CONTENTS.—Sam Huff.—Willie Davis.—Larry Wilson.—Tommy Nobis.—Gino Marchetti.—Bob Lilly.—Joe Schmidt.—Dave "Deacon" Jones.—Chuck Bednarik.—Henry Jordan.—Dick "Night Train" Lane.—Dick Butkus.
1. Football—Biog. I. Title.
GV939.A1A46   796.332'64'0922   67-20384
ISBN: 0-394-80197-0   ISBN:0-394-90197-5 (lib. ed.)

Revised Edition

© Copyright, 1967, by Random House, Inc.

Manufactured in the United States of America

Contents

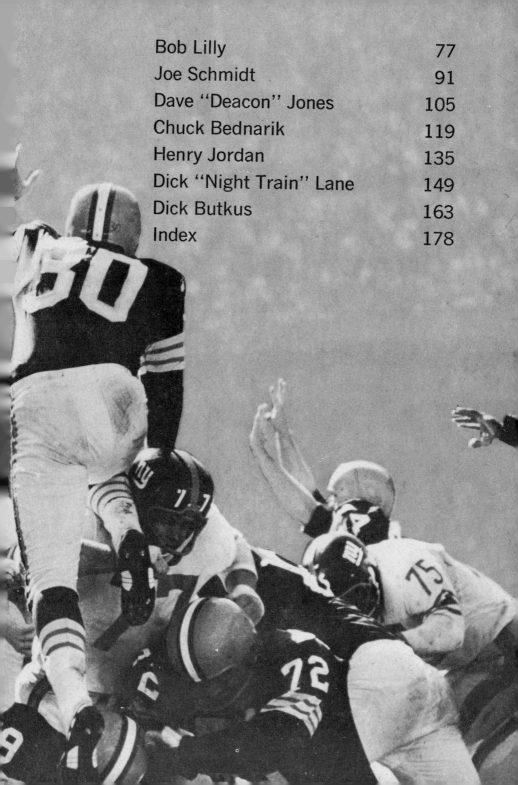

Introduction

Although the players in a football team's offensive unit are often better known, they are not more important than those in the defensive unit.

According to Vince Lombardi, the famous coach of the Green Bay Packers and the Washington Redskins, prior to his death in 1970, "Defensive players have to be tougher, mentally and physically, than offensive players." Lombardi also said, "Championships are won on defense. When I came to Green Bay in 1959, my first moves were designed to strengthen the defense. I started working on developing the offense after that."

Two of the champion Packers—Willie Davis and Henry Jordan—are included in this volume. They personify the toughness that Lombardi talked about. So do the ten other players chosen from among the dozens of superb defensive performers in the National Football League.

Just as the offensive players in the NFL are specialists, so are the defensive players. The ends, for example, must be capable of chasing scrambling quarterbacks, as well as warding off blockers on an end sweep. The tackles, in addition to their pass-rushing ability, must have the strength to stop the powerful line smashes of opposing runners. The linebackers must not only be able to move up and plug the holes on a running play, they must be quick enough to aid in pass coverage when the opposing quarterback looks for one of his receivers. The defensive backs—the cornermen and the safeties—must be almost catlike in their moves as well as courageous enough to tackle the big running backs trying to break past the line of scrimmage.

Willie Davis exemplifies the best in a defensive end, as do Gino Marchetti (perhaps the best of all) and David "Deacon" Jones. Bob Lilly and Henry Jordan represent the tackles. Dick "Night Train" Lane and Larry Wilson represent the defensive backs.

The linebacker has become the glamour player of the defense. Five linebackers are included— Sam Huff, Joe Schmidt, Chuck Bednarik, Dick Butkus and Tommy Nobis. Huff, Schmidt and Bednarik were the players who popularized the position. Butkus and Nobis stand out as the men who carried on the tradition.

In order to appreciate football to its fullest extent, one should understand not only the skills of the offensive players, but those of the defense, too. Whenever an offensive player makes a mistake, or is forced into a bad play, do not blame him. Most of the time, he makes the mistake or the bad play because a defensive player makes a *good* play. As a spectator, learn to appreciate the defensive players. Coaches do.

Great Defensive Players of the NFL

SAM HUFF
Linebacker

From television sets all over the nation the true *sound* of pro football was being heard for the first time by millions of fans. They were accustomed to seeing close-ups of the action—the arching pass, the slamming tackle, the devastating block. But now, on a documentary show titled "The Violent World of Sam Huff," they were listening to the crash and clack of equipment-padded players, and they were hearing the players' voices, too.

"What are you doing there, 88?" growled Sam Huff, who was wired for sound. "You do that once more, 88, and . . ."

Huff, the middle linebacker of the New York Giants, had emerged from a pileup. He was glaring at an opponent wearing uniform number 88. Perhaps more than anything else, the voice of Sam Huff on this 1959 television show made many fans aware of *defense* for the first time, and particularly aware of the position of middle linebacker. People who had seldom noticed the defensive unit before began to appreciate other defensive players on other teams.

On offense, the quarterback is the glamour player. On defense, the middle linebacker is the player most fans watch. The middle linebacker invariably turns up where the action is. When the opposing team uses a running play, the middle linebacker moves up to slam into the ball carrier. On a pass, the middle linebacker either charges at the quarterback or drifts back to cover one of the receivers.

Undoubtedly the most famous of all NFL middle linebackers has been Sam Huff. He was so popular in New York, in fact, that the fans at Yankee Stadium used to chant, "Huff . . . Huff . . . Huff . . ." as he slammed an opposing ball carrier to the ground. When the defensive unit was introduced before a game, Huff always got the loudest cheer. He was selected to five All-NFL teams, and during six of his eight years with the Giants, the team won the Eastern Division title. In fact, Sam Huff symbolized the Giant defense. So much so that it was unthinkable that he would ever be traded. But on April 10, 1964, he was.

The deal, which merited front-page headlines in the New York newspapers, shocked the Giant fans. It also shocked Sam Huff.

Allie Sherman, the Giant coach, had been try-

ing to trade Huff for several days. Sherman be-
lieved that Huff, then 29, was slowing up. The
coach planned to rebuild his defensive unit with
younger personnel. He contacted Tom Landry,
the coach of the Dallas Cowboys. Sherman was
hoping to obtain either defensive tackle Bob Lilly
or defensive end George Andrie. But Landry re-
fused to trade either man.

Sherman and Wellington Mara, the owner of
the Giants, then attempted to work out a three-
way trade with the Redskins and Cowboys. But
that also collapsed, as did another three-way
trade involving the Redskins and the Baltimore
Colts. Sherman then called Bill McPeak, the Redskins' coach.

"Let's make our own deal," Sherman suggested.

"What do you have in mind?" McPeak wanted
to know.

"We'd like to get Andy Stynchula," Sherman
said.

"That depends on who you're offering me,"
McPeak replied.

"How about Sam Huff?" Sherman asked.

McPeak was stunned. He conceded later that
he never would have thought of asking for Huff.
He had assumed that Huff wasn't available.

"For Huff, though," Sherman continued, "we'd
have to have more than Stynchula. Throw in
Dick James."

Playing against his old teammates, Sam Huff (70) blocks a field-goal attempt by New York's Bob Timberlake. The Redskins won, 23–7.

Stynchula was a young defensive tackle. James, a tough little halfback, had led the NFL the previous season in punt returns.

"Let me think about it," McPeak said, trying to hide his anxiety about Huff. "I'll call you back."

McPeak later explained why he wanted Huff. He felt that Sam had presence. He had been with a winning team and had been one of their leaders. That was what the Redskins needed—a player who would not rattle in crucial moments.

Huff, of course, knew nothing of the negotiations. Players are seldom consulted about being traded. During the off-season Huff was working for J. P. Stevens, Inc., a textile firm, and that day he had a business conference in Cleveland. At the Cleveland airport, he came upon Don Smith, the Giants' publicity director, who was en-route to New York. Smith had created Huff's image as a Giant and the two men were good friends. Smith had told the Columbia Broadcasting System that Huff would be the ideal player for their documentary show. And, of course, the show had made Huff famous.

"Smitty," Huff said during their casual conversation at the airport. "You're a good man. If I'm ever traded, I'll take you with me. I'll be the first player ever to take his own press agent with him."

Smith laughed. The Giants never would trade

Sam Huff. But unknown to Smith, at almost that very moment in Washington, Bill McPeak was telling the Redskins' switchboard operator, "Get me Allie Sherman in New York."

Moments later, the trade was official: Huff and a rookie lineman, George Seals, were exchanged for Stynchula, James and a draft choice. The teams agreed not to announce the trade until the following morning. By then, Sherman had informed Huff.

"Even when I heard Allie telling me," Huff said later, "I didn't really believe I had been traded. I guess that was because I just didn't want to believe it. But when I got off the plane from Cleveland the next day and saw the headlines in the newspapers, that's when it began to sink in."

For several weeks, Huff was unable to make up his mind whether or not to join the Redskins. He spoke of the "heritage of victory" that had surrounded the Giant organization and said that he had thought he would be part of that heritage until his career was over. Eventually, however, he signed a three-year contract with the Redskins for a reported total of $100,000. In addition, his contract had a rare clause in it. The Redskins promised *never* to trade him.

McPeak assigned Huff the responsibility of calling defense signals, a job Huff did very well. Immediately he was one of the most popular players, as he had been with the Giants.

Robert Lee Huff was born on October 4, 1934, in Edna Gas, West Virginia. Nicknamed "Sam" by his father, he was the fourth of six children. His father toiled in the soft-coal mines of the Monongahela River valley not far from Pittsburgh, Pennsylvania. But in those Depression years, his father worked irregularly and his mother often had to stand in line at government surplus food centers to obtain flour for baking bread.

"Somehow," Sam recalls, "we always had enough to eat, but it wasn't fancy."

At nearby Farmington High School, Sam was more than a football hero. He was a better-than-average student and an eager participant in the dramatic club. Under his portrait in *The Lincoln-eer,* his senior yearbook, was this tribute:

> *This good-looking boy is our muscleman,*
> *At football he is great;*
> *Sammy used his brains as well as brawn,*
> *He made first team, Class B, All State.*

He also made an impression on college scouts. The University of Florida was interested in Sam. So was the United States Military Academy at West Point, New York. But the Army officials were unaware that Sam had married his high school sweetheart, Mary Fletcher, during their senior year. His marriage made him ineligible to attend West Point. But the most interested college representative was Art "Pappy" Lewis, the coach at West Virginia University.

"That boy is a hunter," Lewis told one of his assistants. "He likes the briar patch. We've got to get him."

In Lewis' language, a "hunter" is a player who enjoys tackling, especially in the "briar patch," the middle of the line. Throughout his career at West Virginia, Huff enoyed the briar patch. At the time, he was a tackle on both offense and defense. He earned several All-America citations, but his teammate, a tackle named Bruce Bosley, was a virtually unanimous All-America selection.

The day of the NFL's annual draft of college players, Huff stopped by the athletic office at West Virginia. He was told that the Giants had picked him on the third round.

"I'm not surprised," Huff said. "I'll make their team, too."

It wasn't quite that easy, though. Huff was selected for the College All-Star team scheduled to oppose the champion Cleveland Browns in August. As a result he was late in reporting to the 1956 Giant training camp. When he did, he seemed confused by the number of assignments he had to learn. The Giant coaches were confused, too. They didn't know where to play him. They tried him at guard, then at defensive tackle, then at offensive tackle.

Huff (70) and teammates gang up on Joe Morrison of the Giants.

"He hasn't fit in any place," Coach Jim Lee Howell told his aides at one of their meetings, "but he's a tough kid. Let's keep him around for the kicking teams and see what happens."

Huff was not aware of Howell's plan. He was discouraged. So was another rookie, Don Chandler, a punting specialist from Florida University. One evening after dinner, Huff and Chandler, who were roommates, made a rash decision. They decided to go home. Sneaking out of the dormitory, they took a taxi to the local airport. At 11:00 P.M., when Vince Lombardi (later the coach of the Green Bay Packers, but then an assistant coach with the Giants) checked the room shared by Huff and Chandler, he discovered their absence.

Hoping they might be at the airport, Lombardi hurried to his car and drove there. He found Huff and Chandler sitting in the waiting room.

"What are you doing here?" Lombardi roared. "What's the matter with you men? Don't you realize that you're going to make this team? Pick up your bags and get in my car. You're going back to camp."

Buoyed by Lombardi's words, Huff and Chandler worked harder than ever at practice sessions. Chandler soon developed into the Giant punter. But Huff had to wait for a chance to prove himself. He had been playing on the "suicide squads" —the kickoff and punting teams. But when Ray

Beck, the middle linebacker, was injured, Sam got his chance. He trotted onto the field in a game against the Cleveland Browns. Seeing the rookie, the Browns assumed they could take advantage of his inexperience.

"Let's run at that number 70," one of the Browns said.

Paul Brown, the coach of the Browns, had the same idea. He sent in plays aimed at Huff. But Huff was everywhere. Play after play, he tackled the Cleveland ball carrier. As he did, the voice on the public-address system at Yankee Stadium boomed, ". . . tackled by Huff . . . stopped by Huff . . . piled up by Huff." Sam Huff was at middle linebacker to stay.

The next season Jimmy Brown joined the Cleveland Browns. As Brown developed into the most feared fullback in football, his duels with Huff became classics. In tackling Brown, Huff liked to hit him low. He would hang on, hoping that help would come. "If you try to tackle him high," Huff said, "he'll run right over your face."

More often than not, Huff, aided by the other alert members of the Giant defensive unit, did well against Brown. But Brown likes to tell of the time that he got in the last word. During one game Huff had tossed the 230-pound fullback for a two-yard loss. As Brown arose, Huff said, "You stink."

On the next play Brown crashed through the

Huff (70) and Giant teammates stop Jimmy Brown.

Giant defense and pranced into the end zone for a touchdown. Turning back to Huff, who had followed him helplessly, Brown said, "Hey, Sam, how do I smell from here?"

Typical of his sense of humor, Huff has always enjoyed telling that story, too. Although a competive terror on the field, Huff is an agreeable personality when he is out of uniform. In 1961 the Packers wrecked the Giants, 37-0, in the NFL championship game. Paul Hornung, who scored 19 points for the Packers, was awarded a sports car by *Sport* Magazine as the game's most valuable player. At the luncheon honoring Hornung, Huff was among the speakers.

"I don't know why Paul Hornung is getting this car," Huff said. "The way the Packers ran through me, *I* was their most valuable player."

Huff hasn't often given a poor performance, however. Not only is he a clever linebacker, he is a rough one. "Football *is* rough," he has often said. "You have to hit ball carriers hard. If you don't, they'll run right by you. That doesn't mean you have to be dirty. There's no reason to punch a player in a pileup or twist his arm or leg. When you do that, you're asking for a 15-yard penalty. And that's the worst thing that can happen, because it hurts your team."

During the 1966 season, Huff was involved in a rough play that injured quarterback Don Meredith of the Dallas Cowboys. In a late-season game in Dallas, Huff caught Meredith behind the line of scrimmage. When Huff tackled him, Meredith went down in a heap. He had been knocked unconscious. He was out for several minutes before wobbling off the field. He did not play again that afternoon and the Redskins upset the Eastern Division champions.

"I wasn't trying to hurt Don," Huff explained later, "but I was trying to tackle him. That's my job."

Huff was always on the job. During his 13 seasons, he missed only four games—all of them in the 1967 season. Quite a few times he played with minor injuries, and his durability was considered remarkable for a middle linebacker.

"He plays every game," said Harland Svare, once coach of the Los Angeles Rams. "Not many guys can say that."

Perhaps the finest tribute to Sam Huff was uttered by a five-year-old girl. One evening after the Giants had lost a game, Giant coach Allie Sherman strolled into his home. His five-year-old daughter, Lori, walked over and kissed him. Then she stepped back and stared at her father.

"Daddy," she asked, "why did you ever trade Sam Huff?"

WILLIE DAVIS
Defensive End

Happy and relaxed in their chartered bus, the Green Bay Packers were rolling toward Friendship Airport outside Baltimore. They had just defeated the Colts, 14-10, and had clinched the 1966 Western Conference title in the National Football League. In the midst of the happy talk on the bus, the voice of Dave Robinson, a Packer linebacker, roared out:

"Willie Davis, I'm sticking with you. Willie Davis, you're going to make me something. Yes, sir, Willie Davis, you are my man."

In the front of the bus, Davis grinned. So did all of his teammates. Among the Packers, the defensive captain was everybody's man.

Davis, who stands 6 feet 3 inches and weighs 245 pounds, was not looked upon quite as fondly by opposing players, however. Storming in from left end, he had a knack for making the big play that wrecks an opposing team. One of these big plays had occurred during the title game in Baltimore.

The Packers were trying to protect their 14-10 lead, but Johnny Unitas, the famous Colt quarterback, had moved his team to a first down on the Packer 16-yard line. With a minute and a half to play, Unitas still had plenty of time to upset the Packers' lead with his passes.

The Colts went into their huddle and Unitas called the play. At the snap, Unitas spun and went back to pass. Realizing his receivers were covered and noticing some running room, he veered upfield. Davis, meanwhile, had been unable to get past any of the Colt blockers. But as Unitas began to run, the big defensive end broke free.

Circling behind Unitas, who was carrying the ball in the crook of his right arm, Davis tackled him high and tugged at the quarterback's right arm. The ball squirted out as if it were a bar of soap.

Dave Robinson pounced on the fumble, and the Packers suddenly had possession of the ball on their nine-yard line. Their triumph was virtually assured. Not far away, Unitas, his face in the mud, his fists clenched in anger, slammed at the slippery turf in disgust. Davis stared at him for a split second before trotting off the field.

"When I saw John lying there," Davis confessed a few weeks later, "I was thinking how I would have enjoyed that fumble a lot more if it had been some other quarterback besides John."

The fumble had provoked a rare emotion in

pro football—sympathy for a defeated opponent.

Willie Davis, however, is an unusual man. He and Unitas, along with Sam Huff of the Washington Redskins, had traveled to Viet Nam the previous winter to entertain United States servicemen. During their tour, the three players had developed a close friendship. But Davis' friendship for Unitas had not prevented him from tackling the Colt quarterback as hard as possible. After the play, though, Davis did not look back at his role in the key fumble with as much enjoyment as usual.

Vince Lombardi, the coach who brought him to the Packers in 1960, often said quite simply that "Willie Davis is a leader." Lombardi respected leadership ability in a player. And to take advantage of this quality in Davis, he appointed him captain of the Packer defensive unit in 1964.

As a captain of his team Davis had a philosophy which made him a source of inspiration to his teammates. "Every time I take the field," he once said, "I want to do the best job I can. And you've got to do your best against the man opposite you on *every* play."

Part of his philosophy was formed in the days following the 1960 NFL championship game with the Philadelphia Eagles.

Toward the end of the game the Packers were leading, 13-10, after scoring a touchdown early in the fourth quarter. But Ted Dean of the Eagles took the next kickoff and bolted along the left sideline to the Packer 39-yard line. With Norm Van Brocklin at quarterback, the Eagles moved to a first down at the 20. But on the next play Van Brocklin was tackled for a seven-yard loss.

The momentum of the Eagles was in jeopardy. If the Packers could stop the next play, Van Brocklin would be faced with a long-yardage situation on third down. Again Van Brocklin went back to pass. Well protected this time, he zipped a quick pass over the middle to fullback Billy Barnes.

Cutting to his left, Barnes chugged to the 14. The Eagles' momentum was restored. Moments later they scored the touchdown that gave them a 17-14 victory.

The next day Willie Davis looked at the films of the Barnes play. And he saw what he had feared. "The play was on the other side of the field," he said. "But if I'd *really* chased him with everything I had, I might have caught him. I was close to him. . . . That was the whole season for me, that one play, and that's all I thought about until we went to training camp in July."

That one play made Davis promise himself that he would give *everything* he had on *every* play. He lived up to this private code from then until he retired in 1970.

Davis was best known, especially among opposing quarterbacks, for his fierce determination.

The Giants' Y. A. Tittle looks worried as Davis closes in on him.

Two who expressed it well are Y. A. Tittle and Billy Wade. Tittle, as quarterback for the New York Giants, had faced Davis twice in NFL championship games. And Wade, during his years as the quarterback for the Chicago Bears, was constantly harassed by Davis.

"Davis," Tittle said, "is a great pass rusher. He is strong and aggressive. He's always towering over you, coming, coming, coming all the time."

"Even if it's only an arm," Wade commented, "Davis finds some way to get in front of you. He's always around you, always putting on the pressure."

Occasionally, though, Willie Davis has a bad game. One unpleasant experience occurred midway in the 1966 season in a game against the Minnesota Vikings. Fran Tarkenton, the Viking quarterback that day, had kept one step ahead of Davis and the rest of the Packer defense during the whole game, and the Vikings had produced a 20-17 upset.

But three weeks later the Packers had their revenge, defeating the Vikings, 28-16. When the game was over, Harry Gilmer, then the coach of the Detroit Lions, looked down from the press box and pointed at number 87.

"Willie Davis," Gilmer said in admiration, "is a one-man gang."

Willie D. Davis (he makes a secret of his middle name) was born in Lisbon, Louisiana, on

Davis is about to tackle Viking quarterback Fran Tarkenton.

July 24, 1934. While he was still very young his parents separated. His mother raised her three children in Texarkana, Arkansas, where Willie attended Booker T. Washington High School. His mother thought football was too rough for her son. But, as a sophomore, Willie went out for the high school varsity team without telling her. Already a solid 170-pounder, he made the team as a defensive tackle and offensive end.

"What about your mother?" one of his teammates asked. "Doesn't she know yet?"

"Not yet," Willie replied. "So far we've played all home games. But next week . . ."

The next week a road game was scheduled. The team wouldn't return home until long after dinner time, and Mrs. Davis would be wondering where Willie was.

Willie asked his coach to talk to his mother before the trip. His coach agreed. He told Willie's mother what a good player her son was and explained that the equipment would protect the boy from injury. But Mrs. Davis kept shaking her head. Eventually the coach surrendered to her wishes. After he had departed, however, Willie pleaded with his mother. Finally she relented.

"All right," she said, hugging him. "But you hurry on home after the game."

Willie glanced at the kitchen clock. The bus was to leave from the high school in a few minutes. Racing out of the house, he ran up the street. The school was not far away, but when he was about a block away, he saw the bus beginning to move. He would have to take a shortcut. He hopped over a fence, through a backyard and across an empty lot. The bus had stopped for a red light. Running up to the bus, he pounded on the door. It opened. He jumped aboard and was on his way to the first road game of his football career.

As a high-school player he was so impressive that he earned a scholarship to Grambling College in Louisana. He was the team captain in his junior and senior seasons.

After starring for Grambling in the Orange Blossom classic against Florida A. & M. in 1955, Davis was selected by the Cleveland Browns in the 17th round of the annual draft of college players. But before he could join the Browns, he was drafted into the Army, where he continued to play ball. He was named to the All-Army and All-Service teams in 1957. But when he finally reported to the Browns, he was merely another rookie trying to make the team. He made it, and that was about all. He didn't play very much during the next two seasons and became discouraged with his lack of progress.

Then, after the 1959 season, Paul Brown, the head coach, told Davis that he would receive an opportunity to play regularly at defensive tackle. As a result he was looking forward eagerly to 1960 training camp.

One early spring day Davis was driving back

to his home in Cleveland when his ears suddenly perked up at the sports news on the car radio.

"The Browns completed a trade with the Green Bay Packers today," the radio commentator announced. "The Browns received A. D. Williams, an offensive end, in exchange for defensive tackle Willie Davis."

Gripping the steering wheel tightly, Davis couldn't believe the news. He thought he had been making good progress with the Browns. He had gained the confidence of his teammates and, he thought, the coaches. But apparently he had been a failure. Now he was going to play with Green Bay.

The previous season, during Lombardi's first year as coach, the Packers had finished with a respectable record of 7 won and 5 lost. But before that they had had a poor record. The Browns, by comparison, had always been contenders for the NFL title. Davis briefly considered retiring, then realized that he would probably get more opportunity to play in Green Bay.

The day Willie reported to the Packer training camp, Lombardi shook hands firmly and motioned him into his private office.

"Willie," the coach said, "I think I know how you feel. You think that the Browns didn't want you. But look at it this way. The Green Bay Packers want you even more. That's why we made the deal for you."

Lombardi went on to explain that the Packers

thought Davis could help them. The coach was aware that Willie had made defensive mistakes, but they were honest mistakes—the type of mistakes all rookies make. "You hustled," Lombardi said, "and you never quit. All I ask is that you play the same way here."

What Lombardi did not say at the time, however, was that he had spotted Davis's ability on game films. Throughout the off-season Lombardi had viewed films of every team in the NFL. While watching the Browns one day, he noticed how Davis continued to pressure the passer. The Browns were using Davis as defensive tackle. But the Packers needed a defensive end.

"This kid is so quick," Lombardi told his assistant coaches, "that he might be even better at end."

Installed at that position, Davis quickly developed into a star. In 1962, he was selected to the All-NFL team, an honor that was repeated in 1964, 1965, 1966 and 1967. Typically, he was annoyed at *himself* when the sports writers failed to select him for All-NFL honors in 1963.

"I realized," he says, "that in this game you can't rest on the things you've done in the past. I thought I had played just as well in 1963 as in 1962, but my name was missing. It woke me up."

Somehow he continued to make discoveries which goaded him into doing his best every game. Unlike many players, he did not have a good game one week, a lesser game the next. He

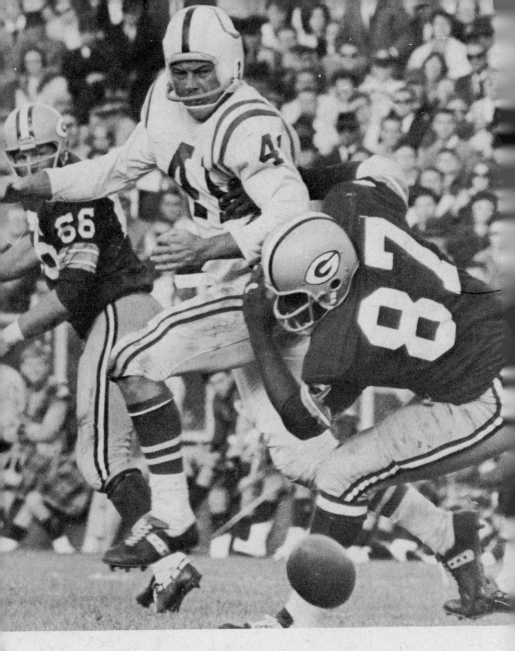

Davis knocks the ball loose from the grasp of Baltimore's Tom Matte.

is consistently spectacular. One day, a few seasons ago, he sat on a stool in front of his locker in the Packer dressing room and explained his thinking.

"I realize that a certain game may mean more than some others at a certain stage of the season," he said, "but I've never thought that you should take it easy one week so you can go all out the next."

It's no wonder that Lombardi selected him to be the captain of the Packer defensive unit. It was an honor Davis took seriously. There was much more to it than merely deciding whether to accept or refuse a penalty, whether to call heads or tails on a coin toss.

"On the Packers," Davis says, "I had to exemplify the kind of approach to the game that will help our team."

When he retired after the 1969 season, Davis' other abilities were recognized. He joined the National Broadcasting Company as a television commentator on NFL games. Early in 1971 he disclosed that he had been offered the prestigious football job as head coach at Harvard University. He turned down the offer since he was too busy with his other business interests.

Someday he may return to football as the coach of a college or pro team. His many fans hope that he'll return sooner rather than later.

LARRY WILSON
Safetyman

One day in the summer of 1965 Buddy Parker, then the coach of the Pittsburgh Steelers, was sitting in a darkened room at his team's training camp. The Steelers were about to play the St. Louis Cardinals, and Parker was watching a film of an earlier pre-season game between the Cardinals and the San Francisco 49ers. Throughout the film, Parker found himself entranced by the actions of Larry Wilson, the safetyman of the Cardinals. Wilson was all over the field, knocking down passes, making tackles and blitzing the 49er quarterback. When the film ended and the lights were clicked on, Parker had an idea.

"Get me a pair of scissors," the coach said to one of his assistants.

Snipping out Wilson's plays, Parker spliced the pieces of film together. The next day he assembled his players and showed them the special film he had prepared of Larry Wilson performing at safety for the Cardinals. When the movie ended, Parker looked around at his team.

"If all you men would only play *half* as good football as Larry Wilson," the coach said, "We'd win every game."

The problem for most of the Steelers, as for most players in the National Football League, is that there is no way they could be half as good as Wilson. He was the most daring pass interceptor in the league. In 1966 he led the league with 10 interceptions. At the beginning of 1971, his eleventh season, he had a career total of 45. In six seasons he had been selected to the All-NFL teams and he was also a member of eight Pro-Bowl squads. More important, he had acquired a reputation as one of the most rugged and respected performers in pro football history.

Retired quarterback Bobby Layne has said, "Larry Wilson is the toughest man in pro football."

At a quick glance, he did not appear to be *that* tough. Weighing 190 pounds and standing 6 feet, he was of average size. His cheeks were slightly hollow. But a closer inspection revealed a whipcord strength that was matched by few players. Unlike most tough players, he did not revel in his ruggedness. Off the field his mild manner did not lend itself to headlines. And even on the field he was not a particularly noisy participant in the defensive huddle. One of his Cardinal teammates, Jerry Stovall, perhaps described him best when he said, "Larry is not a 'holler' guy. He's a 'do' guy."

Wilson (8) intercepts a pass.

As the free safety in the Cardinal defense, Wilson is not always responsible for covering a specific opponent. As a result he is able to roam, covering pass receivers, moving up to tackle big ball carriers and, occasionally, rushing the opposing passer—a daring maneuver for a man of his size. Compared to the blockers he must avoid in order to get at the opposing quarterback, Wilson is small. But the dangers of the "safety blitz" do not intimidate him. If anything, they add to his incentive.

When Wilson charges the quarterback, he attempts to time the snap of the ball, taking a run from five or six yards back. As he comes across the line, he is almost sprinting. It requires courage, because if one of the big linemen, for example a 260-pound tackle, moves out to block him, Wilson is an easy target. He is also a target for the big backs who are blocking in order to give the quarterback time to pass. In a game with the Cleveland Browns, Wilson once leveled quarterback Frank Ryan. But the next time Wilson blitzed, halfback Ernie Green was waiting for him.

"He really popped me," Wilson says. "On the films I looked like a big tree falling."

Although he was carted to the sideline after Green had flattened him, Wilson soon returned to the game. He is not the type to relax on the bench, not even when he has an excuse. His right hand is evidence of his attitude. Normally a person's middle finger is about half an inch longer than the ring finger. But this isn't true of Wilson's middle finger. His is about the same length as his ring finger. It is also bent a little and the big knuckle bulges. Until midway in the 1965 season the finger was normal. Then, in the middle of a game with the New York Giants, he sustained two hand injuries.

He moved up to make a tackle. In the collision he landed on his right hand.

"I lit on the finger," he says, "and for a second all my weight was on it."

At half time he told the Cardinal trainer, Jack Rockwell, that his finger hurt. Rockwell taped it. During the second half, Tucker Frederickson, the Giant fullback, smashed through the Cardinals' line. Wilson came up to stop him. As he tackled Frederickson, his left hand was jammed among the players in the pileup. Pain seared through his hand. When the game ended, the pain was worse. In the locker room he was getting out of his shoulder pads when Jack Rockwell called to him from the trainer's room.

"How's the finger feel now?" Rockwell asked, referring to the right middle finger.

"Never mind the finger," Wilson replied. "You better take a look at my other hand."

That evening X-ray photographs disclosed a fracture of one of the bones across the back of Wilson's left hand. X-ray pictures of the right middle finger revealed another fracture. After reading the X-rays, one of the Cardinal team physicians began to prepare plaster casts for both hands. As the doctor put on the first cast, Wilson glanced up at him.

"Say, Doc," he said, "how about next Sunday? Can I play?"

The doctor stared at his patient. "Play?" he said. "Well, I don't see how you can."

"Why not?" Wilson said. "I can do my job all right."

The doctor shrugged. "Don't count on it," he advised.

Throughout the week, Wilson was unable to button his shirt. His wife had to cut his food for him. But somehow he practiced as usual. The day of the game he strolled into the trainer's room and held out his cast-covered hands.

"All right," the team doctor agreed, "let's try some foam rubber on it and see how it feels."

Rockwell, the trainer, placed a foam-rubber pad over each cast. Then he wrapped adhesive tape around the pads to hold them to Wilson's hands.

"You know what?" Rockwell laughed when he had finished. "You look like a boxer, Larry."

Wilson smiled. His hands appeared to be encased in white boxing gloves. When the game began, he was playing despite the fractures in both hands. Soon he proved that he could do his job as he had told the doctor he could. Leaping high, he enveloped a pass with his "gloves" and

Wilson breaks up a pass intended for Washington receiver Bobby Mitchell.

clutched the ball in his arms. Cradling it against his chest, he returned the interception 34 yards for a touchdown. His play provided the winning margin in a 21-17 game.

He played the next week, too, but after that game the team doctor checked his right middle finger.

"Your finger is sliding," the doctor said. "The bone is actually moving down. Your finger is shorter. The more you play, Larry, the worse it will get. I can't let you play any more. You need surgery."

Wilson surrendered. He missed the next four games, but returned to uniform for the team's final game of the season.

With his hands still protected by the foam-rubber pads, he intercepted *three* passes. He ran back one interception for 96 yards and a touchdown, setting a team record. Several months later, when Charlie Winner took over as the new Cardinal coach, he appointed Larry Wilson the captain of the defensive unit.

"People rally around him," Winner explained. "He gives 120 per cent out there. You don't have to get him up for the game. He's always ready. He is a man of marvelous competitive fibre."

Larry Frank Wilson was born on March 24, 1938, in Rigby, Idaho, then a town of about 1,000 residents. Rigby was not far from the southwestern tip of Yellowstone National Park. When he was 10, his mother died of spinal meningitis. His father, a truck driver for the Utah Power and Light Company, which also services Idaho, never remarried. But he carefully supervised the upbringing of his sons, Larry and John.

"Out in our country," his father likes to say of Idaho, "you've got to have guts. If you don't, you're a nobody."

Larry Wilson was a *somebody*. He starred in four sports at Rigby High School—football, basketball, baseball and track-and-field. He was offered several athletic scholarships, and was going to accept the offer from Idaho State, but his father intervened.

"Take the offer from the University of Utah," his father suggested. "You'll get more national recognition there than you would at State."

At Utah, Wilson was a varsity halfback under two coaches—Jack Curtis for one season, Ray Nagel for two. "Under Coach Curtis," he says, "I learned the fun of the game and under Coach Nagel I learned how important it is to outhit the other team."

As a senior he put together several impressive statistics by gaining 558 yards rushing, 215 yards on 21 pass-receptions, and scoring 84 points. Nevertheless, he was virtually ignored in the All-America polls. The Cardinals, however, were aware of the rawboned runner with the sharp-nosed features. He was their seventh-round draft choice.

When Wilson joined the Cardinals at their 1960 training camp, he was tried at cornerback —but without success.

In his first pre-season game he was assigned to cover Raymond Berry, the star split end of the Baltimore Colts. Berry ran circles around him. The first time Berry caught a pass, he scored on a 40-yard play. The next time, Berry appeared to be on his way to another touchdown when Wilson dragged him down on the one-yard line. Moments later Frank "Pop" Ivy, the Cardinal coach at the time, sent in a substitute. For the next three games, Wilson sat on the bench. One exhibition game remained. Wilson phoned his wife, Dee Ann.

"We're playing in San Francisco this weekend," he told her. "They'll cut me after the game. Meet me in San Francisco with the car and we'll go home together."

In San Francisco, however, his luck changed. One of the Cardinal cornerbacks was injured. In the shuffle of defensive backs, Wilson was started at free safety. He was so impressive that the Cardinals realized he was now playing his proper position. He had obviously been out of place at cornerback. During the next few weeks he established himself as a regular player, as well as the man who was popularizing the "safety blitz." He first used this tactic in a game against the New York Giants.

As he swooped in for the kill, Charlie Conerly,

then the quarterback of the Giants, was startled.

"I'll never forget the look on his face," Wilson says, gesturing. "His eyes popped out to here."

Wilson terrorized quarterbacks with his reckless dash through the line. At a Pro Bowl game one year, veteran Y. A. Tittle, who had starred with both the Giants and the 49ers, said to Wilson:

"I didn't know you were so small. If I had, I wouldn't have been so afraid."

Pass receivers fear Larry Wilson, too. "When he tackles you," says Pete Retzlaff, a long-time star with the Philadelphia Eagles, "you know it. He hits as hard as anybody in the league."

But what the pass receivers most fear about Wilson is his knack for interceptions. When the Dallas Cowboys arrived in St. Louis early in the 1966 season, Bob Hayes, their star split end, was looked upon as the most dangerous pass receiver in the league. But during the game Wilson leaped in the air and snatched a pass right out of Hayes's hands.

"Nobody ever did it quite like that to me before," Hayes said later.

One of Wilson's most spectacular games took place against the Chicago Bears in 1966. He intercepted three passes and was the most outstanding player in the 24-17 victory. The game was televised nationally, the first time a pro-football game had been seen during weekday prime-time. All over the country the next day

Wilson brings down Joe Morrison of the Giants.

people were talking about Larry Wilson. Typi-
cally, he had been banged up during the game.
In the first quarter his left hand was stepped on.
In the fourth quarter he was knocked dizzy.

In the locker room later, blood oozed from the
cleat mark on his hand. His blue eyes were
misty from the head blow.

"I'm all right," he told newsmen. "If you come
out of a game *without* any bruises, you should
be in different work."

Wilson received the game ball that night, the
seventh of his career with the Cardinals. At his
neatly furnished home in St. Louis, the game balls
were on display along with a Cardinal helmet.

"I'm real proud of them," he says in his Idaho
twang. "To me, getting a game ball means everything."

These trophies are merely the physical repre-
sentations of an inward competitive attitude
which makes him excel among other players.

"In football," Wilson says, "you've only got
sixty minutes to prove what kind of a player you
are; forty-nine minutes aren't enough. It might
take eleven more to show somebody that you're
really a great player."

Larry Wilson has probably made more use
of those eleven minutes than any other player in
the NFL.

TOMMY NOBIS
Linebacker

As the Gemini 7 space capsule whirled in orbit around the earth on December 8, 1965, astronaut Frank Borman chatted on radio with the communications men at the Space Center in Houston, Texas.

"And by the way," the astronaut said, "tell Tommy Nobis to sign with Houston."

At the time, Nobis, an All-America linebacker at the University of Texas, had been drafted by both the Atlanta Falcons of the National Football League and the Houston Oilers of the American Football League. Astronaut Borman's interest was understandable. He lived in Houston and rooted for the Oilers. But the astronaut's comment had been unique. No other football player had ever received an "order" from outer space.

Several days later, while astronaut Borman was still in orbit, his radio crackled.

"Bad news," reported the voice at the Space Center. "Nobis has signed with Atlanta."

Borman was silent for a few moments and then he said, "There's no joy in Mudville."

In Atlanta, however, there was much joy. Tommy Nobis had been the first player selected in the NFL draft. It is reported that the Falcon owners guaranteed him a total of about $300,000 in salary and bonuses spread over several seasons. If this figure is accurate, it is a record sum for a rookie defensive player. But the Falcon owners considered it a good investment.

And it has been. During the Falcons' brief history, Tommy Nobis has been their dominant player.

Nobis received a rare honor in his rookie year when he was named to the Eastern Division All-Star squad for the Annual Pro Bowl game. The Falcons won only three games in Nobis' first season (it was also the first season for the Falcons, who had just been established as a new team in the NFL).

"But I wonder if we would have won *any* games if we hadn't had Tommy," coach Norb Hecker said after the season was over.

Except for the 1969 season, when a knee injury limited him to performing in only four of the Falcons' 14 games, the 6-foot-2, 240-pound Nobis anchored their defensive unit. He was selected to an All-NFL team in 1967, and he had been named to the Pro Bowl squad in four of his first five years in the National Football League.

Nobis stops a ball carrier trying to go through the middle of the line.

His most serious rival for All-NFL honors has been his contemporary, Dick Butkus. "But I'd much rather play against Butkus than Nobis," says Larry Csonka, the big running back of the Miami Dolphins.

"The thing about Nobis is that he doesn't get wild-eyed like Butkus does. Nobis has a coldness about him. And if you don't watch out, he'll put you out of the game."

The other Falcons respect Nobis immensely. One of his teammates, running back Harmon Wages, was a lieutenant in the same National Guard unit in which Nobis was a lowly enlisted man.

"When we're on guard duty," said Wages, "I yell 'Attention!' to my platoon, and then I always say, 'If it's all right with you, Tommy.' I don't want that man to get angry at me even if I am the lieutenant."

Despite his success, Nobis did not have an easy rookie year in the NFL. In one of his early games, the Philadelphia Eagles gave him a rough initiation. On their first offensive play, the Eagles' quick halfback, Timmy Brown, began to run a sweep play to his right. Nobis, at middle linebacker, diagnosed the play perfectly and moved out to chase Brown. But he never caught him. The huge Eagle offensive tackle, 275-pound Bob Brown, leveled Nobis with a shattering block.

"I thought the world turned upside down,"

Nobis said later in the locker room. "All I could see was the sky. Man, I'd never been hit like that before."

The play had been part of the Eagles' game plan. They wanted to welcome Tommy Nobis to the NFL on the first play. As Nobis talked about it after the game, two former Eagle heroes, Chuck Bednarik and Tommy Brookshier, consoled him.

"I hurt all over when I saw Brown clobber you with that block," Bednarik said.

"That's like walking along a street and having a truck fall on you," Brookshier said.

Nobis smiled, realizing that the NFL was tougher than college football had been. "In college," he said, "I could get blocked and still have time to make the tackle. Here it's too fast. I kept guessing wrong all day. When I'd blow in there, they ran around me. When I fell back, they threw over me. They had Jim Ringo chopping me down in the second half. I guess Bob Brown told Ringo that anybody could handle me."

In the Eagle locker room, Brown chuckled when Nobis' words were relayed to him.

"We decided to give the young man a baptism," Brown said. "But listen, Nobis is going to be a great one. We just had him confused. I'd hit him from one side, Lane Howell [the other offensive tackle] from the other side. Double trouble. And whenever he played tight, Ringo [the Eagle center] would block him. But Nobis hung in there.

He's got lots of heart. You wait, he will be a great one."

Although Nobis was confused, he still made 14 tackles during that game. That number would prove to be his average throughout the season's 14-game schedule.

Against the Chicago Bears, Nobis made 20 tackles and aided his teammates on 14 others. After that performance Hal Herring, who coached the Falcon linebackers, mentioned that the first things to look for in a great linebacker are size, strength, speed, quickness and the desire to excel. "Nobis," he said, "has all of those things."

Herring also pointed out that of the 46 running plays the Bears had employed, Nobis had participated in 34 tackles.

"He has the things that can't be coached," Herring said. "Size, speed, willingness to listen and learn, dedication to hard practice and improvement. He's popular with his teammates and he realizes that the front four [the two ends and the two tackles] protect him from blockers and give him chances to get at the ball carrier. Operating up and down the line, he knows any one of seven opposing players can take a shot at him. He's taking his licks and dishing them out."

Thomas Henry Nobis always enjoyed the body contact of football. He grew up in San Antonio, Texas, where he had been born on September 20,

1943. When it was time for him to go to high school, his choice was determined by football.

"In San Antonio," he says, "you could go to any high school you wanted to, no matter where you lived. I knew that Jefferson High had the best football coach, Pat Shannon. So I enrolled at Jefferson. It was a little hardship, but it was worth it in the long run."

In order to get to Jefferson High in time for his first class, he had to get up at 5:30 A.M. and ride a bus to the other side of the city. Had he not been so dedicated to football, he could have attended a nearby high school and slept until 7:30 every morning. The greater distance also affected the time he returned home from football practice.

"It was usually around eight o'clock, sometimes eight-thirty," he has said. "It was a long day, but it was worth it."

Indeed it was. He earned All-Texas schoolboy honors. He also learned a tackling philosophy that would stay with him throughout his career.

"Hit those ball carriers right in the goozle," Tommy liked to say. "That's what Coach Shannon told us."

The goozle was Shannon's term for the ball carrier's chest—the target area for all his tacklers at Jefferson High.

As an all-state star, Nobis had several athletic scholarship offers. He narrowed his choice to either the University of Texas or Oklahoma Uni-

versity. He made his decision on the day he
visited the Oklahoma campus.

"Too many people up there were bad-mouth-
ing Texas," he recalls. "So I knew I didn't want
to go to Oklahoma."

Enrolling at the Texas campus at Austin, Nobis
quickly impressed his freshman coach, Pat Cul-
pepper. During his sophomore year in 1963, he
moved into the starting varsity lineup as an offensive guard as well as a linebacker.

While Nobis was a junior, Texas claimed the national championship in the Orange Bowl by upset-
ting the former national champions, the University of Alabama (with Joe Namath at quarterback), 21-17. But Nobis was haunted that season
by a 14-13 loss to Arkansas.

"When we talk about a successful season at
Texas," he said at the time, "we mean winning
them all—9-1 is not successful."

To Darrell Royal, the head coach at Texas, Nobis was something special. "He might well be the
best linebacker in the history of college football,"
Royal said one day while Nobis was playing his
final varsity season. "People talk about the great
ball carriers in college history. You pick any-
one you want and you know what Tommy would
have done to him? He'd have stuffed him, that's
what. All he does every week is play a great game
and you can just see joy on his face when he's out
there. He's done it from the first game he started,

As a University of Texas linebacker, Nobis charges through a hole after intercepting a pass.

which was as quick as I could get him into a suit as a sophomore."

At the time Nobis was on his way to earning unanimous All-America honors, as well as being awarded the Outland Trophy as the nation's outstanding college lineman.

The acclaim was no accident. No matter what the occasion, Tommy Nobis consistently played to his limit on a football field. During the intrasquad scrimmage at the end of spring practice, prior to his final season, he appeared to be everywhere. On one play, he drove a ball carrier out of bounds. On the next play, he tackled another ball carrier on the sidelines on the *other* side of the field. On the next play he intercepted a pass over the middle. In the press box a sports writer asked Jones Ramsey, the sports information director at Texas, why Nobis was expending so much energy in so meaningless a game.

"That's easy," Ramsey replied. "It's the only football game we've got scheduled today."

Nobis himself has often said, "Football is my life. It always has been."

In the days before the annual draft of college players by the NFL and AFL (which were rivals at the time), Nobis was ranked high on every team's list. In the NFL, the new Atlanta franchise had first choice. According to Vince Lombardi, the coach of the Green Bay Packers, there was no doubt about which player the Falcons would take.

"The Number One choice," Lombardi had been saying for months, "has to be Tommy Nobis."

When the Falcons claimed Nobis, it was not a surprise, but it was unusual. Ever since the NFL began its draft in 1936, most of the Number One selections had been quarterbacks or ball carriers or pass receivers. Two centers had been Number One choices—Chuck Bednarik of Penn had been drafted by the Philadelphia Eagles in 1949 and Ki Aldrich of Texas Christian University had been drafted by the Chicago Cardinals in 1939. But Nobis was the first linebacker ever to be chosen as Number One.

During his early days in training camp with the Falcons, he discovered he had to adjust to NFL competition.

"I'm not turning those tacklers around like I did in college," he said. "When I hit them, they're not going backwards like they used to. Half the time they're falling on me. I don't know how to explain it, but I feel as if I'm playing a good game and at the same time playing a bad game. I'm making a lot of mistakes. In college I didn't have to think as much. Pro ball doesn't seem too much tougher physically, but you have to do a lot more thinking and learn a lot more. And you can't relax for a second."

He also found out that the spirit among the

Nobis, in the middle of the action, tries to diagnose the play.

professional players is as strong as among the collegians.

"But it's a different type of spirit," he said. "It's hard to explain. In college you have all those pep talks and that stuff, but in the pros you get ready for a game differently. You know that if you don't produce you're not going to have a job. You feel the other people on your team know what they have to do, so you're just concerned about doing your own particular job."

Tommy Nobis does his particular job so well that he has developed into one of the most spectacular players in NFL history.

He also emerged as a unique player in another respect. Several days before his first Pro Bowl, he was asked to make a television appearance in Los Angeles. One of the television technicians walked over to equip him with a microphone. But when he tried to put the microphone cord around Nobis' neck, he had a problem.

"It won't fit," the television technician complained. "Your neck is too big."

Nobis' neck is, in fact, so large that he must wear a 19½-inch collar. The Atlanta Falcons might be wise to purchase a special television microphone cord for their star linebacker. Nobis will probably be using one quite often in the years to come.

GINO MARCHETTI
Defensive End

One day at the Baltimore Colt training camp, an assistant coach was tutoring a rookie offensive tackle in the art of blocking. Testing the tackle was veteran defensive end Gino Marchetti. At the time, Marchetti was the most feared pass rusher in the National Football League. The rookie bent down into his stance and braced himself for Marchetti's charge.

"Hut, hut," the coach barked, imitating the quarterback's signals.

The tackle lunged forward. But Marchetti grabbed him by the shoulder pads and swept by him. The tackle frowned.

"Lower," the assistant coach instructed. "Get down lower in your stance."

Again the coach barked signals. Again Marchetti shoved the tackle aside and moved toward an imaginary quarterback.

"Lower," the coach repeated. "Get lower or he'll get by you every time."

The tackle crouched as if he were a panther. At the signal, he pounced forward. This time Marchetti put one of his huge hands on the rookie's helmet and leapfrogged over him. The rookie, embarrassed, peeked at the coach.

"What," he asked, "do I do now?"

"Applaud," the coach answered.

Gino John Marchetti was born on January 2, 1927, in Antioch, California, a small town not far from San Francisco. His father, Ernest, had immigrated to the United States from San Jinese, Italy, and had settled with his wife, Mary, in Antioch. Gino grew up in a happy family; one of his few disagreements with his father concerned football. Gino wanted to play for the Antioch High School team, but his father had to give him written permission to do so.

"I don't want you to play," his father said. "It's too rough. You might get hurt."

Finally his father relented, but he kept telling Gino, "When all those players run at you, get out of the way." Gino had to laugh at his father's idea of football, but at least he had received permission to play.

Then one day in 1942, shortly after Gino's fifteenth birthday, three strangers drove up to his house in a car with United States government license plates. His father, who owned a popular tavern, went out to see what they wanted.

"This is a government eviction notice," one of the men said, handing Gino's father a piece of paper. "You've got a week to move to a Federal Security Center."

His father protested, but the government agents explained that they were only doing their duty. Several weeks earlier, Japan had attacked the United States naval base at Pearl Harbor, triggering the entry of the United States into World War Two. Both Italy and Germany were allies of Japan and therefore many people of Japanese, German or Italian lineage were considered "sabotage risks." Gino's father had taken out his citizenship papers, but his mother had not and was technically still an Italian. As a result, the entire family was placed on a detention "farm" in the California countryside.

"Every day my mother cried," Gino once said bitterly. "And every day I thought about how to get even."

Gino concluded that the best way to get even was to prove that the United States government was wrong in regarding the Marchetti family as sabotage risks. On the morning of his eighteenth birthday, Gino appeared at his local draft board to enlist in the Army. Soon he was a machine gunner with the 69th Infantry in Europe. He went through several months of fierce combat. Once he and the other men of his squad were out on patrol when a Nazi tank fired a shell at them.

Everybody in the patrol was killed except Marchetti. Later, in the fighting around the German city of Koblenz, he killed an estimated total of 30 Nazi soldiers. He was also among the first dozen Americans to enter the city after the German troops were driven out.

When word of his battle actions got back to Washington, D.C., the government finally realized that the Marchetti family was not really a security risk. They were permitted to return to their home in Antioch. Gino's father reopened his tavern and in time the family prospered.

Many of Gino's friends believe that the same spirit that made him a war hero is also the basis of his ability as a football player. When he was discharged from the Army, however, he gave very little indication of his future prowess on the football field. He had been out of high school for four years and had made no plans to enter college. His main occupation was tending bar in his father's tavern. His favorite sports were motorcycle racing and semi-professional football. He quickly earned a reputation as the strongest football player in the Antioch area.

One day Brad Lynn, an assistant coach at the University of San Francisco, drove over to Antioch to meet Marchetti in order to confirm the reports on him. He took one look at Gino and invited him to USF for a tryout.

Marchetti put on his leather jacket, "the one

with 15 zippers," he recalls, and jumped on his motorcycle. When he arrived at the sedate USF campus, head coach Joe Kuharich shuddered.

"Get rid of this kid," Kuharich told Lynn. "He's not the college type."

"But Joe," Lynn said, "he's the strongest person you've ever seen."

Kuharich thought a moment; Marchetti surely appeared to be strong. He was 21 years old and stood 6 feet 3 inches tall and weighed 225 pounds. He was a man among boys and just the kind of player Kuharich needed to anchor his defensive line.

"All right," Kuharich said. "As long as he's here, get him some equipment and let's see what he can do."

Kuharich pitted Marchetti against his best players, one on one. Gino handled them as if they were babies.

"You've got a scholarship," Kuharich said, "but do yourself a favor. Don't wear that jacket around here."

Gino agreed not to wear the jacket and in time he even stopped riding his motorcycle. Gino's fondness for motorcycles had worried Kuharich because of the possibility of serious injury.

The University of San Francisco was a good influence on Marchetti, and he soon developed into a polished, mature young man. He developed into a polished, mature football player, too. Out of the men with whom Gino played in college, eleven went on to play in the NFL. Among them were running back Ollie Matson, quarterback Ed Brown and offensive tackle Bob St. Clair.

Marchetti, a defensive tackle at USF, was the Number-Two draft choice of the old New York Football Yankees in 1952. But several days after the draft, the Yankees' franchise was shifted to Dallas, where the team was called the Dallas Texans. Then, after Marchetti's rookie season, the team was moved to Baltimore, where they became the Colts.

Marchetti was moving around in the lineup, too. He wasn't quite big enough to play defensive tackle, so he was made an offensive tackle. But he did not have much success at this position.

Then in 1954 Weeb Ewbank took over as the head coach of the Colts. One of his first decisions was to put Marchetti at defensive end. It turned out to be one of the best moves Ewbank ever made. As Marchetti developed into an All-NFL performer, the Colts developed into NFL champions. Marchetti, of course, was not entirely responsible. The Colt defensive unit had such stars as tackle Gene "Big Daddy" Lipscomb, tackle Art Donovan, linebacker Bill Pellington and halfback Milt Davis. The offensive unit was led by quarterback Johnny Unitas, split end Raymond Berry, halfback Lenny Moore, fullback Alan Ameche, tackle Jim Parker and guard Art Spinney.

Marchetti (89) reaches for a Lion ball carrier.

During the late 1950s, the Colts had one of the greatest teams in pro-football history. Unitas got most of the headlines, but among the players themselves Gino Marchetti was the leader.

Ironically, at the moment of the Colts' greatest glory, Marchetti was not on the field. He was sprawled on a locker-room rubbing table with a fractured left ankle. Typically, though, he had made the victory possible.

The play occurred during the 1958 NFL championship game with the Giants. The Giants were leading in the fourth quarter, 17-14, with slightly more than two minutes to play. They had a third down on their own 39-yard line and needed four yards for a first down.

If the Giants obtained the first down, they would virtually clinch the game. By keeping possession of the ball and not fumbling, they could run out the clock. But the Giants did not make that all-important down. Marchetti, clawing through Giant blockers, stopped halfback Frank Gifford inches short of a first down. When the players unpiled, however, Marchetti was lying on the ground, writhing in pain. His ankle had been broken. He was lifted onto a stretcher and taken to the sidelines.

As a result of Marchetti's tackle, the Giants punted on the fourth down. With one minute and 56 seconds to play, the Colts had the ball on their own 14-yard line. Racing onto the field, the Colt

offensive unit went to work to set up the tying
field goal. With Unitas clicking on short passes,
the Colts moved to the Giants' 13-yard line. The
clock was ticking off the final seconds as place
kicker Steve Myhra ran onto the field. At the
other end of Yankee Stadium, Marchetti was being carried on a stretcher toward the dugout
leading to the Colt dressing room.

"Hold it," Gino said to the men carrying him.
"Let's see this."

Myhra swung his foot and the score was tied,
17-17. There were only seven seconds left to
play. The clock ran out and the game went into
"sudden death" overtime. The first team to score
would win the game—there would be no chance
for the other team to even the score.

After the Colts kicked off, they forced the Giants to punt again. Then, moving methodically
downfield, they scored on a three-yard run by
fullback Alan Ameche and won, 23-17. There
was no doubt that the Colts' opportunity to win
had rested on Marchetti's final tackle.

"Gino, Gino," his Colt teammates yelled as
they clomped into their dressing room. "Gino gets
the game ball."

The game ball is the symbol of victory in pro
football. As his teammates shouted and danced
around him, Marchetti lay on the rubbing table.
Although in severe pain, he was smiling and
clutching the game ball to his hairy chest.

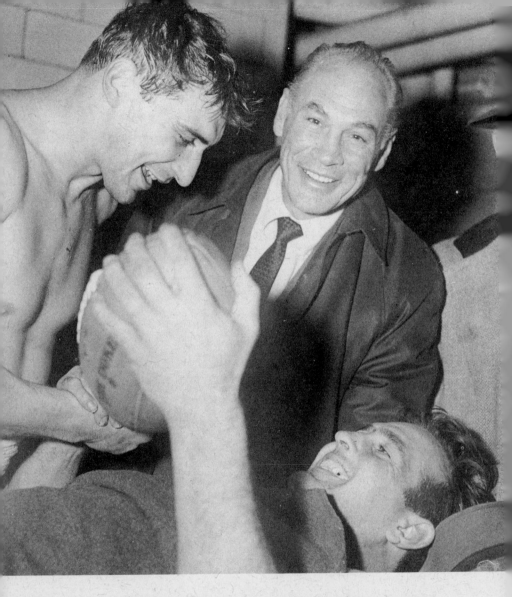

Marchetti holds game ball after the Colts' sudden-death victory over the Giants in the 1958 NFL championship game. Alan Ameche and Colt owner Carroll Rosenbloom are congratulating him.

His ankle, however, bothered him for months. It still wasn't strong when he reported to training camp in 1959, and there were whispers that he had lost his speed and that his career soon would be over. After all, he was 32 years old. But by the time the season opened, his ankle was sturdy again. Marchetti had another big season and the Colts won another NFL title.

Instead of losing speed as he grew older, Marchetti appeared to be gaining some. Three years later he was timed at 4.9 seconds for the 40-yard dash. "He's the fastest lineman we have, offensively or defensively," said Charley Winner, later the coach of the St. Louis Cardinals, but then a Colt aide. "None of them approach five seconds for the 40. But Gino beats it."

Another time Winner was putting the Colt defensive backs through a reaction test. They had to execute certain maneuvers within a 10-yard area. Winner timed them with a stop watch. Marchetti strolled over and watched the backs dash and dart about.

"Say, Charley," he said, "let me try that."

Marchetti ran through the obstacle course and his time was faster than that of any of the defensive backs. "And defensive backs," Winner pointed out, "are supposed to be the quickest people on your team."

Marchetti was as hard as oak. At six-feet-four and 253 pounds, he was big, although not as big as many defensive ends. But his quickness and agility made him something special. The Detroit Lions once charted him in a game. "He never made the same move twice," said George Wilson, the Lion coach at the time. "Nobody else has that kind of imagination."

"He was the best defensive player I ever had to go against," quarterback Bobby Layne once said. "People always ask me what it's like to be tackled by Marchetti. Did you ever run into a tree in the dark? Well, compared to Gino, that's like running into a pillow."

Marchetti received another tribute one day from Buddy Parker, who was coaching the Pittsburgh Steelers. Parker was sitting in a darkened room watching movies of a Colt game. He kept rerunning a play that puzzled him. Marchetti, a big 89 on his white Colt uniform, had slammed through to tackle the ball carrier for a three-yard loss. The quarterback also went down in the pileup.

"Are there two Colts wearing 89?" Parker asked. "Or is Marchetti tackling both the ball carrier and the quarterback?"

"Of course Marchetti's tackling both of them," one of the assistant coaches laughed. "He's got two hands, hasn't he?"

Movies of Marchetti in action were often required viewing for players as well as coaches. George Halas, the coach of the Chicago Bears,

*During a game with Green Bay, Marchetti stops
both Jim Taylor and tackle Forrest Gregg.*

once ordered defensive end Doug Atkins to study
Marchetti. Atkins terrified quarterbacks, too, but
he realized that he could learn something new
by watching Marchetti, who was considered a
master of defense.

"Here I go," Atkins often said on his way into
the film room. "Another chapter of 'The Gino
Marchetti Story'."

After the 1963 season, Marchetti announced his
retirement. But when Colt owner, Carroll Rosenbloom, asked him to play in 1964, he agreed. He
also returned for four games in 1966 prior to his
final retirement.

"It was the first time Carroll ever asked me to
do something for *him*," Gino said at the time. "I
couldn't refuse him. Not after what he had done
for me."

A few years before, Rosenbloom had helped
Marchetti and two Colt teammates to establish
a chain of drive-in restaurants, thus assuring
Gino of a substantial income after he retired from
football.

Of course, Marchetti, in his turn, had done a
great deal for Rosenbloom and the Colts. During
his thirteen seasons with the Colts he had helped
them to win two NFL championships and three
Western Conference titles. For nine consecutive
years he had been selected as a defensive end on
the All-NFL team. This record of selection to the
All-NFL team began in 1956 and ended in 1964

and is unmatched by any other player.

On the day of Marchetti's final home game in 1964, he and teammate Bill Pellington, who also was retiring, were feted with a "Day" in their honor. Among the guests were Ernest and Mary Marchetti, Gino's parents. Their air fare from California had been paid through the contributions of Colt fans, because Gino's parents had never been able to attend a Colt home game.

When Gino stood at the microphone to make his speech, he pointed to his parents.

"I want to thank you fans for getting my mother and father here," he said. "That's something I couldn't do."

When the ceremonies ended, Gino escorted his parents off the field. His father, looking around at the capacity crowd of 60,213 spectators, who were cheering his son, shook his head and said, "Gino, maybe you did know how to play football after all."

BOB LILLY
Defensive Tackle

Having thundered across the field on an end
sweep, Jimmy Brown of the Cleveland Browns
was running along the sidelines. Suddenly Bob
Lilly, the 6-foot 5-inch, 225-pound defensive
tackle of the Dallas Cowboys, lowered his shoulders and smashed into the feared fullback. The
two of them careened out of bounds. Brown, perhaps the best ball carrier in the history of the
National Football League, sprawled and skidded
toward his team's bench. His orange helmet momentarily disappeared.

"Lilly took his head off," said a sports writer in
the press box. He hadn't really, of course. But
throughout his career Jimmy Brown seldom had
been tackled as fiercely as Bob Lilly did on that
cool October day in 1964. When the game was
over, several sports writers spoke to Lilly about
the play. His shaggy, straw-colored hair glistened
with sweat as the big Cowboy thought about the
question.

"Four years ago," he said, thinking of his rookie season, "I might have missed him completely."

"Why would you have missed him then?" one of the writers said. "What was different then?"

"As a rookie you haven't developed pride in yourself," Lilly replied. "As a rookie you tend to look up to too many people. You hate to hurt their feelings because you think they'll make you regret it. But now I couldn't care less. That's their tough luck. There's not a better feeling in the world than to come across the field at full speed to let someone have it, even Jimmy Brown. That's football."

In the Browns' locker room, another sports writer reminded Jimmy Brown of Lilly's tackle.

"He hits hard," Brown said with a smile, "a lot harder than a lily. He's more like a thorn."

Perhaps a better comparison would have been a cement tower. More than any other player, Lilly anchored the defensive unit of the Cowboys in their rise to the 1970 National Football Conference title.

Entering the 1971 season, Lilly was rated the best defensive tackle in the NFL. He had been selected to the All-NFL teams for seven consecutive seasons.

His qualifications were best described early in the 1965 season by Tom Landry, the coach of the Cowboys. Landry had a sheet of statistics which showed that his defensive ends had bro-

Lilly charges through a hole in the New York Giants' line.

ken through their initial pass blockers 80 times during the previous season. Another sheet showed that his defensive tackles had broken through their initial pass blockers 180 times.

"From that," someone said to Landry, "your tackles are more than twice as good as your ends."

"But you've got to remember," Landry said, "that Bob Lilly makes all these figures look a little silly."

Landry, one of the most respected defensive minds in pro football, went on to explain. "What throws these figures out of whack is that Lilly *always* broke through his first block. *Always.* And sometimes through the second and third blocks. There is no one man in football who can contain Lilly. When a man breaks through that first block, there's a good chance that he's either going to get to the passer or run into a second block and make it easier for someone else to get to the passer."

Quite often Lilly penetrated the opposing pass blockers to nail the quarterback himself.

One of his most spectacular games as a pass rusher occurred during the 1966 season. The Cowboys, struggling to overtake the St. Louis Cardinals in the Eastern Division race, were playing in Pittsburgh. On the two previous Sundays the Steelers had upset the Cardinals and another contender, the Browns. In the fourth quarter, the Steelers still had a chance to upset the Cowboys.

The Cowboys were leading, 13-7, but the Steelers had intercepted one of Don Meredith's passes deep in Steeler territory.

As the Cowboy defensive unit trotted onto the field, the players knew their job: keep the Steelers pinned down. Some of Lilly's teammates were yelling, "No first down, no first down."

Moments later the Steeler offensive unit hustled up to the line of scrimmage, the 17-yard line. The Cowboys were aware that the Steelers might try to use halfback Dick Hoak on an option run-or-pass play. Hoak had run for 14 yards on such a play in an earlier touchdown drive. The week before, Hoak had thrown a touchdown pass on the option play.

"Hoak, Hoak, watch Hoak!" one of the Cowboy linebackers shouted as the Steeler quarterback, Ron Smith, called signals.

At the snap Smith spun and pitched out to Hoak, who was running to the left. Suddenly, Lilly loomed in Hoak's path. After barreling through the Steeler guard assigned to block him, Lilly had his arms out as if to smother Hoak. The Steeler halfback did not hesitate. He stopped and ran the other way. But after taking a few steps, Hoak realized that he was trapped. Jethroe Pugh, the other Cowboy tackle, had smashed through on that side.

Desperate now, Hoak retreated, hoping to find running room. But Lilly and Pugh converged on him at the five-yard line.

Lilly traps Packer quarterback Bart Starr before he can pass.

"I thought the whole Pitt Stadium fell on me," Hoak said later. "Pugh is tough enough, but Lilly is just too much."

The Cowboy defense, led by Lilly, had destroyed Pittsburgh's hopes on that play. The Steelers were forced to punt. The Cowboys soon clinched a 20-7 victory and were on the way to the divisional title.

Although Lilly's pass rushing is spectacular, he finds more enjoyment in pursuing a ball carrier across the field.

"Watching the game films," he says, "it's nice to see yourself make a good tackle. And it's fun when you get to the passer. But what gives us all a great feeling is seeing everybody hustling after a man in the open."

Robert Lewis Lilly was born on July 26, 1939, in Olney, Texas. The town is located in the oil fields and is not far from Abilene. Out on those flat plains, there isn't much for a boy to do except eat and play football. Bob Lilly did both well. Growing tall and powerful, he was a hero at Throckmorton High School as both an offensive and defensive end. Oddly enough, though, he was playing volleyball on the day that Allie White, an assistant coach at Texas Christian University, first saw him.

"Who is that big kid?" White asked a bystander.

"That's the Lilly boy," he was told. "Pretty good athlete around these parts."

"Does he play football?"

"Like he was three men."

Jotting down the information, White returned to TCU. He knew that Lilly had another year to go in high school. Therefore he would have to wait until Lilly was ready to graduate before approaching him about entering TCU. But prior to his senior year at Throckmorton, Lilly moved to Pendleton, Oregon, where his father had obtained a job as a bulldozer operator in the forest ranges. Lilly had no trouble making the high-school team in Pendleton. He was named to the All-America schoolboy squad.

One day at TCU, Allie White was thumbing through the All-America schoolboy lists and noticed Lilly's name.

"Once a Texas boy, always a Texas boy," White said to another TCU aide. "Maybe we can still get him. I'll write him."

Several weeks later, White received a reply. Bob Lilly was indeed interested in attending TCU. But the day he reported to White, he appeared pale and tired and he had lost quite a few pounds. When the coach asked him if he was ill, Lilly replied that he had just traveled non stop nearly 2,000 miles from Oregon. He and a friend had driven the distance in Lilly's old jalopy, eating only the sandwiches and lemonade prepared by Lilly's mother.

The next day, however, Lilly reported to freshman practice, refreshed by several hours of sleep and a couple of steaks. Abe Martin, the head coach at TCU, inspected the newcomer's powerfully muscled frame.

"He looks like a good one," Martin said, nudging White, "if he's got the desire."

The "desire"—or drive, or hustle, as it is often called—is always a big question with any athlete. But Martin soon discovered that Bob Lilly had come to play. In later years the coach would say that Lilly "has more equipment and ability than any boy I've ever coached—and he gets the *most* out of it."

Another important factor in his career at TCU was his aggressiveness. "He was great at recovering fumbles for us," White says. "That proved his aggressiveness. To recover a fumble, you have to be aggressive enough to stick your head in there and fight for the ball."

As a tackler, Lilly was even more impressive. In a game against the University of Texas during his junior year Lilly, in his purple TCU uniform, moved out to stop an end sweep. Jimmy Saxton, an All-America that year for Texas, was galloping behind a convoy of three blockers. But Lilly, as Coach Martin later recalled, "cleaned out the blockers with one move and got Saxton with the other."

Martin chuckled and added, "After that, people around here called him 'The Purple Cloud.'"

Some of Lilly's classmates held him in awe,
too. One day, having nothing better to do, one of
them noticed a parked Volkswagen. Pointing to
Lilly's huge biceps, the classmate wheedled him.

"If you're so strong," he said, "let's see you
lift that VW onto the sidewalk."

After sizing up the little car, Lilly, without rolling up his sleeves, lifted the rear end onto the
sidewalk. Then walked around to the front end
and lifted that onto the sidewalk. His classmates
shook their heads in disbelief. But afterward,
this tale of Lilly's power became more exag-
gerated day by day.

"It got so that some people were saying that I
put the car up on the library steps," he says now
with a laugh. "I'd have needed a crane to do
that."

Lilly's feats, both on and off the football field
at TCU, had been well charted by the Cowboys.
The TCU campus is in Fort Worth, only a few
miles from Dallas. The Cowboys, naturally, knew
all about Lilly. Their problem in the annual draft
of college players was how to obtain him. They
had traded their Number One draft choice. And
Coach Landry realized that without a Number
One choice, the Cowboys would need a miracle
to prevent another team from selecting him on
the first round.

During the day of the draft Landry was glanc-
ing at his list of college prospects, when Paul

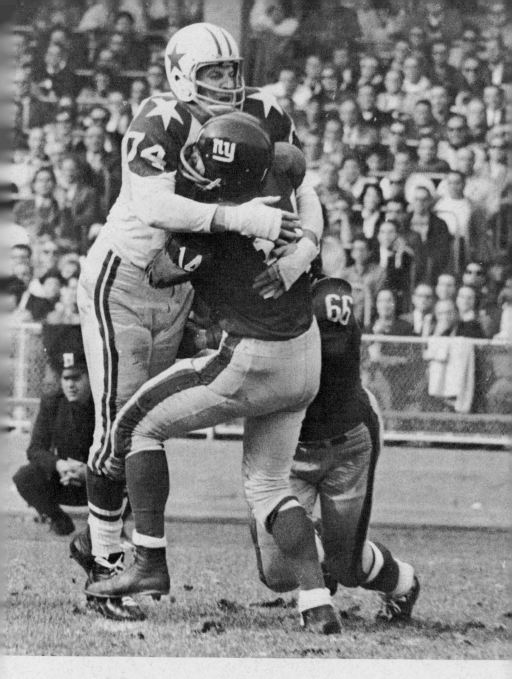

Lilly envelops Giant quarterback Y. A. Tittle.

Brown, then the coach of the Cleveland Browns, walked over to him.

"Tom," Brown said, "I've got a problem. We wanted to take Jim Tyrer, the Ohio State tackle, as our Number One, but we've just learned that Tyrer has signed with the Dallas Texans [now the Kansas City Chiefs] of the American Football League.

"I'll make a deal with you," Brown continued. "I'll give you our first-round choice if you give me that tackle you have, Paul Dickson, and your first-round choice for next year."

"It's a deal," Landry said.

After Brown had received approval for the trade from NFL Commissioner Pete Rozelle, Landry stood up and announced, "Dallas selects Bob Lilly, tackle, of Texas Christian, following a trade with Cleveland."

"Oh, no," moaned a man from the Philadelphia Eagles.

"What's wrong?" Landry said, looking around at the people in the Eagle delegation.

"Lilly was going to be our pick," the Eagle man said.

Landry smiled and sat down. He knew only too well that the Eagles were to make the next selection. The miracle had occurred. The Cowboys had obtained Bob Lilly.

During Lilly's first few seasons, however, Landry began to fear that Lilly had not been a wise choice. As defensive end, the position to which he had been assigned, Lilly floundered. For more than two seasons, he was a disappointment.

"Then I realized," Landry said later, "that Lilly's temperament was not suited to defensive end."

Switched to tackle, Lilly was an instant star. The reason, as Landry explains, "is that at end, Bob had to be more disciplined in his thinking than he is at tackle. On defense, end is a very confining position. Lilly relies so much on his physical talents—his great quickness, agility, balance, strength—he can be out of position and still get back to make the play. He couldn't take advantage of all his talents at end."

Perhaps his most important physical talent is his quickness in "slithering past a blocker," as his teammates describe it.

Bob Lilly has another talent, too—the proper mental approach to his task. Day after day he studies game films of the guards who are assigned to block him. He also maintains his physical condition throughout the off-season with lively games of handball in a gymnasium not far from his Fort Worth home. And even when he is relaxing, he is often squeezing a hand exerciser.

On or off the field, Bob Lilly is always thinking about the game of football—to the dismay of his opponents.

JOE SCHMIDT
Linebacker

In January, 1967, Joe Schmidt took over as the coach of the Detroit Lions. His appointment was announced by the club owner, William Clay Ford, at an elaborate press conference in the team offices. After Ford introduced him, Schmidt told the newsmen of his plans to improve the Lions, then he asked if there were any questions.

The sports writers asked several serious questions about the various problems of the team. Then there was a lull. After a short silence, one of the newsmen, winking at a companion, asked, "Joe, do you think you can find a middle linebacker as good as you were?"

Schmidt smiled self-consciously. Ford laughed and commented, "That's an unfair question."

Although it had been asked in jest, the question was indeed unfair—not only for Joe Schmidt, but also for every defensive player on the Lions. It is doubtful that any of the current Lions will equal the prestige and the popularity that Joe Schmidt attained. Few players in the history of the National Football League, in fact, have earned the respect of their teammates and opponents as Schmidt did.

"If I were to start a team from scratch and had my pick of one player," said Norm Van Brocklin, then the coach of the Minnesota Vikings, "I'd select Joe Schmidt to form the core of my team."

When the Lions possessed one of the most feared defensive units in the game a number of· years ago, Schmidt *was* the core. The defensive captain, he was selected for eight All-NFL teams and nine Pro Bowl squads. He was somewhat small for a middle linebacker, standing 5 feet 11 inches and weighing 215 pounds, but he was nevertheless a terror on the field.

"He's a great tackler and a strong leader," Vince Lombardi, then coach of the Green Bay Packers, often said, "and he can diagnose plays in an instant."

Although Schmidt was extremely effective as a team leader and as a defensive signal caller, he derived his greatest enjoyment from the crashing physical contact of tackling an opponent.

"Hearing the 'pop' of your shoulder pad or hearing the ball carrier grunt is a pretty sound," Schmidt says. "It's the one real joy in this game."

In explaining his tackling technique, he always said that it was "necessary to hit a man low in the legs. Particularly when a back has two or three steps on you and he's coming at you full speed. If you don't get low enough, he'll run right over you. Try to hit him around the knees, his thighs at the highest. I try to get as low as I can and knock his feet out from under him."

*Schmidt stops John Henry Johnson cold during a
1956 game with the 49ers.*

One of his most spectacular tackles occurred in a game with the Chicago Bears. After bursting through the middle of the line, Bobby Watkins, a Bear halfback, suddenly somersaulted in mid-air. Schmidt had hit him low and Watkins had flipped into the air. When he landed, he was facing the other way.

Although Schmidt was a brutal tackler, there was nothing brutal about his nature. In a game with the Baltimore Colts, one of the Lions whacked Johnny Unitas across the bridge of the nose. Stunned by the blow, Unitas tumbled to the ground and was semi-conscious for several seconds. As he rose to return to the huddle, he wobbled. Schmidt, who was nearby, noticed that Unitas was quite groggy.

"Kneel down," Schmidt said to him.

"Let him fall," another member of the Lions growled. "Let him collapse."

"Kneel down," Schmidt said again.

Gently, he held one of Unitas's arms while the Colt quarterback sank to one knee and rested for a few moments until his head cleared.

"I've never forgotten that," Unitas says. "It was quite a gesture."

In the midst of the action, Schmidt had remembered to care for an injured opponent. Nobody had to tell him to do it, he simply did it because that was his nature.

Nobody had to tell him what defensive formations to call in the Lion huddle, either, because

defensive formations had become as much a part
of his nature as sympathy for a groggy player. As
the leader of the defensive unit, he had the responsibility for selecting the proper alignment
from among five basic formations, with possibly
50 variations for each formation. In addition, he
had to be aware of several related items, all of
which entered into his battle plan: the yard line,
the distance to the sideline, the down, the yardage the opposing team needed for a first down,
the time and the opposing players—the quarterback, his runners and his receivers and which
plays they have been favoring.

In a matter of seconds Schmidt had to put all
this information together, as if he were a com-
puter, and designate the defense.

"And after I did that," he once said with a
laugh, "I had to think what *my* responsibility was
on the formation I'd just called. Every once in a
while I'd get caught on a quick snap and I'd blow
my assignment."

Not often. During the 1961 season the Lions
charted every play and, out of a total of 890
plays run by the opposing teams, Schmidt made
only seven mistakes in judgment or execution.

In addition, his signal-calling in anticipating
opposing plays was virtually flawless. In a game
with the New York Giants in 1962, Y. A. Tittle, a
master quarterback, placed himself behind the
center to call signals.

"46, 31 . . ." Tittle began.

Ron Kramer of Green Bay doesn't look at all surprised as he is dragged down by Joe Schmidt.

Schmidt, glaring at Tittle from across the line of scrimmage, shouted, "Blue, blue," changing the Lion defense.

"Check," Tittle yelled, changing his team's play, "74, 32."

"Red, red, red," Schmidt shouted, alerting the Lions to a different defense.

"Time out," Tittle snapped.

Schmidt had diagnosed the plays and out-foxed Tittle. As the Giants retreated to a new huddle, some of the Lions laughed at Tittle's frustration.

Schmidt was hard on his teammates, too. Once, when Alex Karras was a rookie defensive tackle, he joined the defensive huddle with a suggestion.

"Why don't we use the red defense?" Karras asked.

"Quiet!" Schmidt snarled. "You've been here for six games and you want to call the defense? Quiet down."

"Yes, sir," Karras said.

Another time the Lions were losing to the San Francisco 49ers, 24-7, in a play-off for the 1957 Western Conference title.

"It's too bad I'm playing with a lot of quitters," Schmidt roared at his teammates at the half. "What a bunch of dogs."

Jolted by his words, the Lions rallied to defeat the 49ers, 31-27. The next week their fervor continued in a victory over the Cleveland Browns in the NFL championship game. The significance of Schmidt's angry words, however, is that the other Lions accepted his criticism.

"The reason for that," one of his long-time teammates once said, "is that Joe has everybody's respect. No player would take that from a man he didn't respect."

Joseph Paul Schmidt was born on January 18, 1932, in Pittsburgh, Pennsylvania. He first became aware of football when he was six years old. His older brother, John, played for Carnegie Tech. Every so often John would bring home a few of his teammates.

"They'd sit around talking football," Joe recalls, "and I'd listen."

His listening was good training. His brother was the center on the Carnegie Tech squad that played in the 1938 Sugar Bowl game. Several years later, John coached the St. Clair Veterans, a semi-pro team composed mostly of men who had served in World War II. At the time young Joe was 14, but he already was good enough to be a tackle on the team. One Sunday the squad traveled by bus to a coal-mining town, where they opposed a team with an ex-college halfback who was 26 years old. Early in the game the halfback smashed into Joe, but Joe held onto him and wrestled him to the ground.

"I didn't think you'd stop *that* guy," his brother told Joe later. "I think you might make a good football player."

Although the other players received a few dollars a game, young Joe never got a cent. John wisely was protecting his younger brother's amateur standing. Joe was happy just to be playing football.

Unfortunately, his junior high school had no team. But two years later he transferred to Brentwood High School. His first day there he sought out the football coach, Al Cevar, and requested a tryout.

"Have you played football before?" Cevar asked.

"Yes, sir," Schmidt said. "Some sandlot football."

Thinking that he meant pickup games instead of the strong semi-pro competition Joe was accustomed to, Cevar shook his head.

"This will be a lot tougher," the coach said. "I don't know if you ought to come out. You're already 16 and a junior."

"But I'd like to give it a try," Joe said.

Reluctantly, Cevar agreed. During the next few days, the coach soon realized that he had a real football player in Joe Schmidt. In order to take advantage of the teenager's speed, the coach put him at fullback. Joe was so outstanding that he earned a scholarship to the University of Pittsburgh.

At Pitt the coach converted Joe into a linebacker, but his career was interrupted continually by injuries. As a freshman he fractured two ribs.

As a sophomore he suffered a fractured wrist and a shoulder separation. As a junior he had knee trouble. As a senior he spent 10 days in a hospital, recovering from a concussion.

One day during his senior season a Pitt teammate named Richie McCabe, who worked as a water boy for the Pittsburgh Steelers of the NFL, took Joe to a Steeler practice session.

"Mister Rooney," McCabe said to Art Rooney, the owner of the Steelers, "this is Joe Schmidt."

"Oh," Rooney said, shaking hands with Schmidt, "you're the kid who gets hurt all the time."

Those words hurt Joe much more than any injury he had suffered. Rooney's statement meant that Joe's hometown Steelers apparently were not interested in selecting him in the annual draft of college players.

The Detroit Lions, however, knew nothing of Schmidt's history of injuries. When their scout, Buster Ramsey, saw him pile up ball carriers in the Senior Bowl game at Mobile, Alabama, he began to ask about Schmidt. He soon heard the story that most people like to tell about Schmidt's days at Pitt.

The Panthers were about to play Notre Dame in 1952. Their coach, Red Dawson, left the locker room so the players could talk among themselves. Schmidt strode to the middle of the floor.

"We're going to whip Notre Dame," he roared, "or so help me, I'll whip all of you."

Pitt won, 22-19, and later one of the Pitt players confided to a friend, "We were more scared of Joe than we were of Notre Dame."

Anybody with that much desire, the Lions thought, was worth drafting. The Lions won the NFL championship that year, a development that, ironically, discouraged Schmidt. For he thought that he had a chance to make the Steelers, who were not in the running for the NFL title. But the Lions seemed much too good for him to be able to make the team.

"I don't think I'll bother going to their training camp," he told his brother John.

"Don't be silly," John replied. "Go up and try it. You have nothing to lose, Joe."

Schmidt drove to the Lion camp outside Detroit with Gene Gedman, a rookie halfback from the University of Indiana. He had played with Gedman in the Senior Bowl. When they arrived, Nick Kerbawy, then the general manager of the Lions, made a big fuss over Gedman, but he virtually ignored Schmidt.

"And when I saw the size of the veterans in camp," says Schmidt, "I really wondered what I was doing there."

Despite his insecurity, he played fiercely. In his first scrimmage, he intercepted three passes. In another he flattened Vince Banonis. As he stood over Banonis, Schmidt feared that the veteran guard would be angry. Instead Banonis got up and slapped Schmidt's rump.

Green Bay's Bart Starr doesn't have a chance to pass as he is smothered by Schmidt.

"That's the way to hit, kid," he told the rookie. Schmidt made the team. His first two seasons he was used as an outside linebacker, while Les Bingaman, a whale of a man weighing 350 pounds, performed at middle guard. In 1955 the concept of pro defensive formations changed. The middle linebacker, a player who had to protect against passes as well as running plays, replaced the stationary middle guard.

"Schmidt is our man," Buddy Parker, the Lion coach, decided. "He can move and he can hit."

He soon emerged as the most popular player on the team. When the Lions won the 1957 championship, hundreds of fans surrounded him on the field at Tiger Stadium. A few hoisted him onto their shoulders and carried him off in triumph.

Five years later, on Thanksgiving Day, when the Lions submerged Packer quarterback Bart Starr with overwhelming pass rushing, the fans again lifted Schmidt onto their shoulders and paraded him to the locker room.

"I remember Joe Schmidt," says Starr. "It seemed like he was looking inside my helmet. He knew exactly what I was thinking."

Coach Don Shula once said, "Joe Schmidt was a great player because he worked at it. He studied off the field. And he had great desire on the field. He wanted to be a great player. And he was."

Joe Schmidt now wants to be a great coach. And he intends to work just as hard as he did as a player.

DAVE "DEACON" JONES
Defensive End

At the end of a 1966 game between the Los Angeles Rams and the Detroit Lions, both teams were walking back to their adjoining locker rooms in the Los Angeles Coliseum. David Jones was a few steps ahead of Lion quarterback Karl Sweetan. Throughout the game Jones, the huge defensive end of the Rams, had smothered Sweetan's attack and the Rams had won, 24-3. As the players neared their locker rooms, Sweetan noticed Jones ahead of him. Sweetan made a sour face, looked up at the back of the 6-foot 5-inch, 255-pound Jones and stuck out his tongue.

Players for both the Rams and the Lions laughed at Sweetan's playful gesture. When the sports writers arrived a few minutes later, several players told them about it. One of the writers decided to check with Sweetan.

"Sure, I did it," Sweetan said, smiling, "but I made sure his back was turned."

Even off the field, quarterbacks do not want to take a chance on arousing David "Deacon" Jones.

The nickname "Deacon" was given to him by his teammates at South Carolina because he was in the habit of leading the team in prayer before a game. Once, several opposing players noticed Jones kneeling as he prayed.

"What's *he* praying for?" one of them asked.

"That he doesn't kill anybody," he was told.

Jones is one of the most feared pass rushers in the NFL. Entering the 1971 season he had been selected to the All-NFL teams seven years in a row. Jack Christiansen, then coach of the 49ers, once said, "Jones is *the best* defensive end."

Jones's size is a factor in his success, but there have been many other big players who have not been able to match his accomplishments. Perhaps his most important asset is speed. He has been clocked at 9.8 seconds in the 100-yard dash, an amazing time for a man of his dimensions. In addition to his speed, he has agility, a talent which quarterbacks have learned to regret.

In a game against the Green Bay Packers, Jones swooped in on quarterback Bart Starr and tossed him for a loss of yardage four times. The Packers pride themselves on their ability to protect the passer. If Starr is dropped for a loss once in a game, it is a noteworthy event. But Jones had done it by *himself* four times.

"He was in on me so quickly," Starr said later, "that I thought he was one of my own backs."

In a game with the Cleveland Browns Frank

After avoiding Zeke Bratkowski's blockers, Jones
tackles him shoulder-high during a game with
Green Bay.

Ryan, the Browns' quarterback, called a roll-out play. Ryan was to take the snap, then run wide to the right and look for flankerback Gary Collins on a pass return. When Ryan arrived at the spot where he was to look for Collins, Jones was roaring toward him. Seconds later Ryan was on his back.

"C'mon," Ryan said to Jones, "tell me you were hiding out here all the time waiting for me."

Jones had to laugh. At times he has aroused laughter in other players, too. Once, just as Mark Woodson, a speedy halfback for the Pittsburgh Steelers, appeared to be breaking into the clear, he was hauled down from behind by a Ram with a big 75 on his blue-and-white jersey.

"Oh, no," Woodson said, thinking it might be Jones, "say it's not you."

"It's me, it's me," the Deacon said, "the only man who could catch you."

On another occasion, Bobby Mitchell, one of the fastest pass receivers in the NFL, was dashing along the sidelines. Jones angled in on him. Instead of tackling him immediately, however, Jones ran with Mitchell stride for stride for a few yards before bumping him out of bounds.

"What were you doing?" Ram coach Harland Svare later asked on the sideline. "You let him get extra yards."

"Sorry about that, Coach," Jones replied. "But I just had to find out if I was as fast as Mitchell. And I was."

Although Jones possessed marvelous individual ability, he was even more effective because he was a member of one of the NFL's most respected defensive lines—the original "Fearsome Foursome." Next to him was left tackle Merlin Olsen, standing 6 feet 5 inches and weighing 276 pounds. At right tackle was Roosevelt Grier, 6 feet 5 inches and 296 pounds. At right end was Lamar Lundy, 6 feet 7 inches and 263 pounds.

"We are so tall," Grier has said, "that when we stand at the scrimmage line or go running in with our arms up, the quarterback needs a step ladder to see over us. And we are so heavy that we would flatten a Cadillac if we climbed on the roof."

Their size not only impressed opponents, but it made the Fearsome Foursome very popular among the Los Angeles fans. Ordinarily, such offensive stars as the quarterbacks, ball receivers and pass receivers receive the applause at a game. But in Los Angeles, as in many other NFL cities, the defensive stars have developed into favorites of the fans.

Such popularity has surprised some of the older players, who remember when they toiled anonymously. After a gallant goal-line stand one day, the big crowd at the Los Angeles Coliseum cheered loudly as the defensive unit trotted to the sideline.

"What's that yelling for?" one of the Rams asked.

"It's not for the Baltimore offense," Jones quipped.

Although the Deacon received much of the individual acclaim among the members of the Fearsome Foursome, he was quick to credit the entire unit for his personal headlines.

"We work well together," he said. "We have our own signals. We let each other know what we are going to do."

In the defensive huddle Jones, Olsen, Grier and Lundy formed their battle plan according to the game situation.

"Maybe one is going to rush inside, so the other rushes outside," Jones said. "Maybe two are going to fire in, so the other two lay back. Of course, things usually go differently than you plan them. You've got to change what you start out to do sometimes. But we have played together long enough now so that we know instinctively how one of us is going to react to something. And we always cover up for each other."

Of the four, Jones was the least known as a college player. Olsen at Utah State, Grier at Penn State and Lundy at Purdue were All-America performers. The Deacon was grateful just to attend South Carolina State.

David Jones was born on December 9, 1938, in the little town of Eatonville, Florida, not far from Orlando. He has two brothers and five sisters. His father, Ishmael, worked as a carpenter

Jones is about to spoil a pass by Milt Plum of the Detroit Lions.

and a gardener, but he had a hard time support-
ing his family.

"We did not have much," the Ram star once
said, "and we did not have much to look forward
to."

His parents, however, impressed him with
the fact that he must go to college.

"College," his father often told him, "is your
gateway to success. We'll help you as much
as we can, but you'll have to help yourself. Save
the money you make at jobs after school. If you
want to go to college badly enough, you *will* go."

At the time David was a hero at Hungerwood
High School, where he competed in football,
basketball, baseball and track-and-field.

One day a man representing Mississippi Vocational College in Itta Bena, not far from Green-
ville in the northern part of the state, offered him
an athletic scholarship.

"And the best part," the man said, "is that
you'll be able to play on the varsity teams as a
freshman."

At the larger colleges, a freshman is not eligi-
ble for varsity competition until his sophomore
year. But Mississippi Vocational had such a
small enrollment that freshmen were permitted
to play.

"The scholarship is wonderful," his father said,
"but you'll have to make your own spending
money."

"Don't worry," David told his father. "I'll get

it. I'll get jobs. I'll do anything to go to college."

And he did just about anything. He worked as a waiter, a busboy, a bellboy, a short-order cook, a chauffeur, a handyman.

"I even worked as a butler," he says. "All the money added up. It certainly was worth it to me."

After his freshman year at Mississippi Vocational, he transferred to South Carolina State, in Orangeburg. There he completed his education while leading the football team. In addition to his defensive work, he played offensive end. He once caught a touchdown pass on a 75-yard play. But it was his aggressiveness and agility which impressed the Rams' scouts. Oddly enough, though, they discovered him by accident.

During the 1960 season two Ram scouts, Eddie Kotal and Johnny Sanders, were studying college game films.

"I want you to see this halfback," Kotal said, mentioning a player who was on the team playing against South Carolina State. "I think the kid has a chance."

As the reel of film spun, however, the halfback was tackled repeatedly by a huge player on the South Carolina State squad.

"Never mind the halfback," Sanders said. "What's that big kid's name? He looks like the best player on the field."

Several weeks later the Rams chose David Jones in the 14th round of the annual draft of college players. That summer, before he reported to training camp, one of his hometown friends teased him that he wouldn't make the team.

"Maybe not," David replied, "but I'm going to give it my best shot. This is my chance to be somebody."

As Jones says now, "If I hadn't made it in pro football, where would I have gone? What would I have done? You don't get anything in life without working for it, without sacrificing for it. I literally took hold of the one rung on the ladder that was open to me and hauled myself up."

But his first grip on the ladder was shaky. The Rams already had two established defensive ends, Gene Brito and Lamar Lundy. Luckily, the team was not as well staffed at offensive tackle. When one of the assistant coaches asked Jones what he thought was his best position, Jones replied that he played best at offensive tackle. He had decided that he would never get a chance at defensive end.

Within a few weeks, however, Brito was hospitalized, and Jones was shifted to defensive end. When the season began, Jones was in the starting lineup. He has been a regular ever since. But while he was playing, he also was learning. When Harland Svare took over as the Ram coach in 1962, he was stunned by Jones's inexperience. The first time he saw Jones settle into a three-point stance, a fundamental of football, he shook his head. When the drill ended, he called Jones aside.

"Who taught you *that* stance?" Svare asked. "Nobody taught me," Jones replied, "I just sort of picked it up as I went along."

"It looks it," the coach said.

Svare began to work daily with Jones on his stance. "Before Svare corrected me," he says, "I used to get up clumsy out of my stance. When those blockers would blast-block me, whooompff, I was helpless. I couldn't get anywhere with someone's head in my gut. And when I tried to jump around them, the quick ones would ride me so far out of the play I needed a ticket to see the game. But Svare changed me around so my stance was comfortable and I could hit the blocker first and get by him before he could hit me and take the speed out of me."

But just as important, Jones was willing to learn. "David wanted to work on it," Svare said at the time, "and in addition, he had fantastic talent."

The combination created an All-NFL defensive end. Some pro football people compare Jones to Gino Marchetti, but Jones himself disagrees.

"Marchetti was beautiful," Jones says. "He was the only perfect defensive end. Perfect, perfect."

In 1963, however, nobody compared Jones to Gino Marchetti. He had arrived at training camp almost 40 pounds overweight. He thought the added weight would help him. Instead, it detracted from his quickness. The Rams considered trading him, but fortunately, they decided against

Jones stops fullback John Henry Johnson of the Steelers.

that. Even though he weighed 290 pounds, he was spectacular often enough for the Rams to believe that he would regain his form as soon as he returned to his proper weight. The next season he arrived at training camp weighing 250 pounds.

"I learned my lesson," he said. "You've got to play at the weight that lets you do the most."

During the 1964 season he was a terror on the field. He was credited with 79 unassisted tackles, a high total for a defensive end. But when he is on the field, he actually weighs much more than the 255 pounds listed in the game program. The reason: he uses virtually all the protective equipment that is available.

"I wear everything I can get my hands on," he says. "Including hand pads. But I still get beat up."

Usually the opposing players are more battered though. Jones likes to begin the game by hitting ball carriers hard. "Put that shoulder into them a few times right away," he says, "and it sometimes takes the brave out of 'em."

Quarterbacks are his pet target. But he dislikes the scrambling type of quarterback. A scrambler requires a defensive end to chase him all over the field. This is an advantage for the smaller, shiftier quarterbacks. But the quarterbacks who stand and pass from their pocket of pass blockers are his favorites.

"I'll always get to that kind," he says.

And those quarterbacks know it, too.

CHUCK BEDNARIK
Linebacker

Head high, hands on his hips, linebacker Chuck Bednarik, the defensive captain of the Philadelphia Eagles, gazed at the Green Bay Packers in their huddle. He checked the ball on the Eagle 20-yard line and then glanced at the scoreboard, which showed the Eagles ahead, 17-13. Bednarik realized that there would be time for only one more Packer play in the 1960 NFL championship game.

One more play. If the Packers scored, they would win. If the Eagles held, Philadelphia would win.

"Whatever you do," Bednarik snapped, turning to the Eagle defensive backs, "cover that end zone. Cover for the touchdown pass."

The Packers hopped out of the huddle and quarterback Bart Starr moved up behind the center.

The 67,325 spectators in Franklin Field were on their feet, exhorting the Eagles with cries of,

"Hold that line! Hold that line!" At the snap the crowd hushed. Starr moved back to pass. He looked toward the end zone, but the Eagle defensive backs had the deep Packer pass receivers covered. Frustrated, Starr looped a short pass to fullback Jim Taylor. It was up to Taylor to batter his way into the end zone. And it was up to the Eagles to stop him.

One of the defensive backs, Don Burroughs, moved up and hit Taylor low. But Burroughs bounced off the Packer fullback. Another Eagle, linebacker Maxie Baughan, also hit him low, but Taylor continued to churn. He was approaching the 10-yard line when Chuck Bednarik closed in on him.

"I saw our guys hitting him low and bouncing off," Bednarik explained later, "so I told myself, 'I'm not bouncing off. I'm bearhugging him high and I'm not bouncing off.'"

They collided at the 10-yard line. Bednarik, 6 feet 3 inches tall and weighing 235 pounds, wrapped his huge arms around the 6-foot, 215-pound Taylor and for a moment neither of them moved. But a second later Taylor crumpled to the ground. Bednarik, still holding fast, fell on top of him.

The whistle blew, ending the play, but the clock was still running. Bednarik made no move to let Taylor up. Suddenly, the final gun went off. The Eagles were the NFL champions. Bednarik then began to untangle himself.

Bednarik (60) pulls down a Giant runner.

"All right, Taylor," he said to the Packer fullback. "You can get up. It's all over and *we* are the champs."

In later years, Chuck Bednarik often would think of the time he tackled Taylor to clinch the NFL championship for the Eagles. "That," he likes to say, "was the play to remember."

Charles Phillip Bednarik was born on May 1, 1925, in Bethlehem, Pennsylvania, an industrial city about 60 miles north of Philadelphia. His parents had journeyed to the United States from Czechoslovakia, but instead of finding their fortune, they found poverty. Chuck's father worked in the steel mills, but sometimes he worked only one day a week. In order to provide heat for their small home, Chuck and his father would go out into the nearby woods and chop down trees for firewood. To get the logs home, they had to attach a chain to them and drag them for several miles. It was a weary way of life for a boy, but it had its compensations.

"All that tree chopping and chain pulling," Chuck said years later, "built up my body for football."

In those days he played football with a stocking stuffed with rags. But one day his father put 25 coffee-bag tops in an envelope and mailed them away for a football that the coffee company was offering as a premium. "That ball lasted two years," Chuck once said, "and it was the thing that changed my life."

At the time, Chuck was about to graduate from elementary school, but he had made no plans to enter Bethlehem High School. Instead he intended to get a job to help his parents. One of his teachers, Paul Trozell, had other ideas, however.

"Go to high school, Chuck," he told the husky youngster. "You'll need a high-school diploma to get a good job. And you can play football in high school, too."

Chuck agreed. His father had been working more steadily, and Chuck realized that eventually a high-school diploma would be worth more to his family than the few dollars he could earn as a school dropout. He tried out for the high-school football team and made the varsity as a freshman fullback. Then one day something happened which changed the course of his career: the team's all-star center was declared ineligible to play because of failing marks.

"Chuck," Coach John Butler said to his freshman fullback, "take this football home and practice snapping it. You're going to be our new center."

In the next game Bednarik played center. He played at that position throughout his high-school career and earned honorable mention on the All-Pennsylvania team. But, ironically, basketball and baseball were his best sports at the time. He made the second team on the All-State basketball squad. And as a baseball catcher he was so good that he had several college scholarship offers.

But upon his graduation, there was no time for college. World War II had begun, and Bednarik enlisted in the Air Force. Soon he was in Europe as a waist gunner on a B-24 bomber. He flew 30 combat missions, earning six Air Medals and five battle stars.

When the war ended in 1945, Bednarik's ideas about school had changed. He now *wanted* to go to college. The GI Bill of Rights guaranteed his tuition, but he needed advice. So he visited his former high-school coach, John Butler.

"Why don't you go down to Penn?" Butler said. "I'll call Coach Munger and tell him you're coming."

Dressed in his Air Force uniform, Bednarik jumped into his old car and drove to the University of Pennsylvania campus in Philadelphia. He arrived at lunchtime.

"Have some lunch at our training table," one of Munger's aides said. "The coach will be right in."

Bednarik, a brawny 230-pounder, sat down with what he later described as a "bunch of kids." Most of the varsity players were teenagers a year or two out of high school. Bednarik towered over them. When Coach George Munger arrived, he stared at the huge Air Force veteran.

"Are *you* Chuck Bednarik?" Munger asked.

"Yes, sir. John Butler sent me to see you," Chuck said.

Munger smiled. "Take the entrance exam," the coach said.

Bednarik passed the exam and began a college career which sparked Penn to some of its greatest seasons. His best season was in 1947, when the Quakers went undefeated with eight victories and a tie. He earned his headlines the hard way, as a linebacker and a center. But he once scored a touchdown in a game against Columbia by scooping up a blocked punt and running 22 yards into the end zone. He was so overjoyed that he tossed the ball into the stands.

During his years at Penn, he was named to a total of 33 All-America teams. Coach Munger described Bednarik as "capable of being an All-America at *any* position." As a senior in 1948, he was awarded the Maxwell Trophy as the nation's outstanding college player.

That year the Eagles were the NFL champions, and they had what was known as the "bonus" selection in the annual draft of college players. They picked Bednarik, making him one of the few linemen ever named as the Number One choice. The day he signed his first Eagle contract, Earle "Greasy" Neale, then the head coach,

Bednarik, playing center, blocks for an Eagle teammate.

warned him, "You're good, but in this league you'll be going against players who are as good and sometimes better. It won't be easy."

Bednarik realized this, but he was willing to take the chance. However, during his rookie year the Eagles had two veteran players in the positions Bednarik usually played: Vic Lindskog at center and Alex Wojciehowicz at linebacker. At the start of the season, Bednarik was on the bench while the veterans played. Bednarik fumed.

"Coach," he said to Neale one day, "I'm not used to sitting on the bench. I want to play football. If not with the Eagles, then with some other team. If you don't want to play me, trade me."

Neale liked Bednarik's spirit. But Lindskog was too good to bench. Not long after, though, Lindskog was injured and Bednarik took over at center. The Eagles went on to defend their title successfully and Bednarik earned Rookie of the Year honors.

After the 1949 season Wojciehowicz retired and Bednarik moved to linebacker, where he soon was an All-NFL performer. In 1954 he moved back to center again, where he played until 1960. Then one day at the Eagle training camp at Hershey, Pennsylvania, defensive coach Jerry Williams called him aside.

"Chuck," Williams said, "I'd like you to practice with the defensive unit once in a while. Just

in case something happens to any of the linebackers."

Williams' fears were realized shortly after the
season began. One of the linebackers, John No-
cera, was injured. This meant that there were
only three healthy linebackers, with none in re-
serve. Then on the first play of the next game another linebacker, Bob Pellegrini, hobbled to the
sidelines with an injury. Buck Shaw, who had
replaced Greasy Neale as head coach, turned to
Bednarik and motioned him off the bench.

"Get in there and go both ways," Shaw said.
"But don't try to be a hero. If you get tired, let
me know."

Bednarik took over at left linebacker. When
the ball changed hands and the Eagle defensive
unit trotted off the field, Bednarik did not go with
them. He waited for the offensive unit to join
him.

"It was a strange feeling," he often said, "to
have ten guys go off and ten guys come on and
me stay out there."

Bednarik experienced that feeling for the rest
of the season and the Eagles put together a nine-
game winning streak to dethrone the New York
Giants in the Eastern Conference. In the NFL
title game with the Green Bay Packers, he
played 58 minutes and made the winning tackle.
After the game, coach Buck Shaw sat in his office
adjoining the locker room and told reporters,

"Bednarik held us together on offense and defense. We've got to thank the old pro."

By playing as both a defensive linebacker and as an offensive center during 1960, Bednarik had achieved his finest season. Although he was the only player in the league to play nearly 60 minutes every game, he felt that there were many other players who had the endurance to play both ways. He cited Rosey Brown of the Giants and Jim Parker of the Colts, who were two of the finest offensive tackles in the NFL. He felt that they would be just as effective as defensive players. And he once speculated on the terror that Cleveland's great fullback, Jimmy Brown, would have created in the hearts of opposing quarterbacks if he had also played on defense.

Bednarik's 1960 season was marred by an unfortunate and much misunderstood incident that resulted in a severe brain concussion for Giant halfback Frank Gifford. It happened during a late-season game with the Giants at Yankee Stadium. The Eagles were leading, 17-10, and they had to win the game in order to remain ahead in the Eastern Conference. The Giants, however, were moving into scoring range during the final minutes.

Then Giant halfback Frank Gifford swung out for a pass from quarterback George Shaw and caught it near the sideline at the 31-yard line. As Gifford turned to race upfield, he noticed Bed-

Chuck Bednarik (60) crashes into Frank Gifford (16) in the famous tackle that knocked the Giant halfback out of the game.

narik coming at him. But he was distracted by Eagle defensive back Don Burroughs, who was only four or five steps away and closing rapidly. At that moment, Bednarik crashed into Gifford at full speed. The impact lifted Gifford off the ground and threw him down on his head.

The tackle also dislodged the ball and an Eagle player fell on it for the recovery. Bednarik raised his hand in triumph and began leaping in the air with joy. Behind him, Gifford lay unconscious. Some of the Giant players and most of the Giant fans assumed that he was gloating over the fallen Gifford. But, as Bednarik later explained, he wasn't aware that Gifford had been injured. He was leaping with joy because the fumble had practically assured the Eagles of the 1960 Conference title.

Gifford, after a few critical hours in the hospital, later absolved Bednarik of using brutal tactics. Gifford called the tackle an "unfortunate accident." But for months thereafter, Bednarik was reminded of the incident by nasty letters and phone calls from unforgiving fans.

After the Eagles won the NFL title, Bednarik talked about what the title meant to him. "It's worth a lot of extra money," he said, "but the money isn't the big thing. The pride is."

Several months later he was selected to be the first recipient of the John Wanamaker Athletic Award as the "athlete bringing the most credit to Philadelphia and his team." At that time he was talking of retirement, but he played two more seasons.

By the time he finally did retire in 1962, he had played for 14 seasons in the NFL and had been selected to eight All-NFL teams and to eight Pro-Bowl squads. He was virtually indestructible, playing in 168 out of a possible 172 regular-season games.

In St. Louis on a December day in 1962, the team trainer stood by him as he took off his Eagle uniform for the last time. The trainer took the white-and-green jersey with the big "60" on it, the white pants, the green stockings, the black cleats, the green helmet with the white eagle wings. They were mud-streaked and soaked with sweat. The trainer put them all into a big box.

"What's all this about?" a bystander asked.

"They're going to the Hall of Fame," the trainer said, referring to the National Pro Football shrine at Canton, Ohio.

"You're going to clean them, aren't you?"

"No," Bednarik said. "They want them just like they are. That's something, isn't it? My uniform in the Hall of Fame."

Hall of Fame officials had anticipated Bednarik's eventual election and did not want to risk losing the uniform. Their actions were justified, because in 1967 Bednarik was elected a member of the Hall of Fame.

HENRY JORDAN
Defensive Tackle

One by one, the veterans of the Green Bay Packers were arriving in the locker room of Lambeau Field for the first day of training camp. A small group of rookies watched as the old pros entered what had been their second home through three consecutive NFL championship seasons in 1965, 1966 and 1967.

"Hey!" One of the rookies chuckled quietly. "I wonder who that old man is."

Not far away sat Henry Jordan, his bald head shining. He did indeed look older than the others, and he had heard the rookie's remark.

Winking at another veteran, Jordan whispered. "I'll show him who that *old* man is."

Because of his premature baldness, Henry Jordan was older in appearance than the other Packers. Actually, he was younger than his roommate, quarterback Bart Starr. Among all the Packers, veterans and rookies alike, he was perhaps the youngest in enthusiasm. As the right tackle of the defensive unit, he was one of its anchormen, as well as its humorist. He particularly enjoyed poking fun at Vince Lombardi, the disciplinarian who coached the Packers.

"Coach Lombardi is very fair," Jordan often said at banquet speeches. "He treats us *all* like dogs."

Jordan was not a mountain of a man. Although he was 6 feet 2 inches tall and weighed 240 pounds, he was smaller than most defensive tackles, who sometimes stand 6 feet 5 inches tall and weigh 290 pounds.

To compensate for his relative lack of bulk, Jordan depended on his quickness. Perhaps the most famous example of his agility occurred in a game with the Baltimore Colts.

As the Colts came out of their huddle, Jordan's adversary, guard Jim Parker, trotted toward him and got down in his three-point stance. Among pro football linemen, games tend to be played on a man-against-man basis rather than team against team. And over the years Parker has often frustrated Jordan. "Jim Parker is the strongest man in football," Jordan had stated. "He's so strong that when he's got his arms up blocking, I could chin myself on them."

Parker, 6 feet 2 inches and 275 pounds, peered through his face mask at Jordan. Behind Parker, quarterback Johnny Unitas barked signals. At the snap, Unitas moved back, looking downfield. Jordan lunged at Parker and their equip-

Henry Jordan puts pressure on Cleveland quarter-back Frank Ryan.

ment collided with a sharp clack. But Jordan did not surrender to Parker's strength. Instead, he surprised Parker. Rather than trying to knock him down or attempting to go around him, Jordan squirmed between Parker's legs.

Parker was amazed. "He went right under me," the Colt guard liked to say, shaking his head. "Right *under* me. Nobody else ever did that to me before."

It's unlikely that any other defensive tackle could have done it.

In another game Jordan's size indirectly prompted one of his most spectacular individual efforts. He was playing for the Western Division All-Stars in the 1962 Pro Bowl. Throughout the game he was operating alongside Doug Atkins, the mammoth 6-foot 8-inch, 280-pound defensive end of the Chicago Bears. When the Eastern Division All-Stars lined up for a field-goal attempt early in the game, Atkins nudged Jordan.

"Little man," Atkins said, "you get out here at end and I'll play tackle. Maybe you can squeeze through and block it."

After they switched positions, Atkins blasted the opposing guard. But Jordan was unable to get through in time to block the place kick. On an extra-point try later in the game, they again switched positions. Again Atkins slammed into the guard, but Jordan missed. The third time, the Eastern Division was preparing for another extra

point when Atkins and Jordan switched. Seeing
Atkins across from him again, the opposing guard
pounced at the big Bear.

"He was going to pop Atkins," Jordan recalled
with a smile, "even though he [the guard] was
offside."

But when the guard leaped, he left a huge
hole. Jordan quickly squirmed through it.

"I was in there so fast," Jordan said, "I had to
wait for the ball to be kicked to block it."

The blocked extra point proved to be the difference in a 31-30 victory for the West.

"And guess what?" Henry said. "They gave *me*
a big trophy as the most valuable lineman."

Henry Jordan liked to play himself down. But
it wasn't easy. He was a defensive tackle on four
All-NFL teams and a member of three Pro-Bowl
squads. He was also among the most popular
players in the NFL. Most of his opponents readily
praised him.

"There's no tackle in this league," said Jim
Parker, "with Henry's moves."

Another Jordan booster was Darrell Dess, a
guard with the New York Giants.

"Henry's so quick," Dess said, "it's hard to
block him. He just gets by you."

One reason for Jordan's popularity was that he
did not belittle his opponents. In his conversation, flavored by his Virginia background, he used
the word "fish" quite often. To him, a fish is a

Jordan closes in on Ram quarterback Bill Munson.

player who can be outsmarted easily. He even applied the term to himself occasionally.

"I looked like a fish on that play," he has said in viewing films. "See how they hooked me."

But when he spoke of opponents, he never gloated over a poor performance. Jordan had a deep professional respect for every player on an NFL roster. Off the field, he never said anything to make them look bad. In uniform, however, he had a different attitude. Then it was his *job* to make them look bad.

Henry Wendel Jordan was born in Emporia, Virginia, on January 26, 1935. His father was a car inspector on the Chesapeake and Ohio Railroad. Henry grew up with three brothers and two sisters. His family was descended from a mixture of French, English, German and Indian ancestors. When he was six, the Jordan family moved to Newport News, Virginia.

By the time he was 13, he was as tall as he was with Green Bay and weighed almost as much. He wanted to play football.

"Sorry, son," his father told him. "You've got baby bones. You're big, all right, but you're not strong enough yet. Your strength hasn't caught up to your size."

One day during the next season Romie Hamilton, the line coach at Warwich High School, spoke to Henry in gym class.

"Are you coming out for football this year, Henry?" Hamilton asked. "We'd like to have you on the team."

"I want to, Coach," Henry said, "but I'm going to have to check with my father. He may not want me to play."

"If you don't," Hamilton said, "the kids are going to start thinking that you're a sissy, you know."

That evening Henry asked his father again. This time his father agreed. Henry joined the football squad. Although he was big for his age, he was the team's smallest lineman. "That was the time of the Korean War," he explains, "and we had fellows coming out of the service to finish high school. We had some big ones."

But the best one was Henry Jordan. When the football season ended, he joined the wrestling team. He was the best wrestler, too. At the age of 16 he won the state's Amateur Athletic Union heavyweight title, wrestling against men twice his age. During one meet he had an amusing experience when an official noted his bald head. Henry was almost as bald then as he was as a pro.

"Aren't you a little old to be wrestling?" the official asked. "This is a strenuous sport."

When he moved on to the University of Virginia, he continued to wrestle as well as play football. He won the Atlantic Coast Conference title in a match with Mike Sandusky of the University of Maryland. Earlier that season Sandusky, who later played with the Pittsburgh Steelers, had defeated Jordan three times. But in the conference championship, Jordan was the victor. In 1957, during his senior year, he was the runner-up for the national collegiate wrestling championship.

One day early in his senior season he received a phone call from Dick Gallagher, the personnel scout of the Browns. Gallagher asked him if he was interested in playing football for the Browns. Jordan replied that he hadn't thought too much about playing pro ball. The football season at the University of Virginia was not over yet, and he would be wrestling during the winter. He told Gallagher that he had even been asked to become a professional wrestler. Gallagher was worried about the wrestling offer, but Jordan assured him that he was more interested in playing for the Browns.

Several days later, the Browns chose him on the fifth round of the draft. After playing with the College All-Stars in August, he joined the Browns. According to Jordan, "By that time all the other rookies had been cut, so I was safe."

Actually, the Browns realized that he was a good player. But his size baffled the coaches. Their problem was to discover his proper position.

Shuffled from offensive tackle to guard to defensive tackle to defensive end, he had no opportunity to establish himself. During that time he was being used on the "suicide squads"— the special teams which participate in kickoffs, punts, kickoff returns and punt returns. In his second year, the Browns continued to move him around. He was a player without a position.

But when Vince Lombardi, who had been the offensive coach of the New York Giants, took over as the head coach at Green Bay in 1959, one of his first actions was to negotiate a trade for Jordan. Lombardi had been impressed with Jordan's brief performances in games against the Giants. On the day training camp opened, Lombardi and his defensive aide, Phil Bengston, called Jordan aside.

"You're our right tackle on defense," Lombardi said.

"But I thought I was too small to play defensive tackle," Henry replied.

"We don't think you are," Lombardi said. "You've got the moves."

"Play tackle the way *you* want to," Bengston added. "You'll do fine."

For the first time, Jordan not only had a position, he also had a first-team job. Not that he was a star immediately. Lombardi and Bengston worked with him extensively during the 1959 season. Strangely enough, even an opposing

Henry Jordan goes after Dallas fullback Don Perkins.

player gave him good advice. The player was Art Spinney, a guard with the Baltimore Colts. After Jordan's first game with the Packers that season, he was strolling off the field when Spinney walked up beside him.

"Henry," said Spinney, "you've got a lot of possibilities, but you're doing some things wrong."

Jordan didn't know what to say. No opponent had ever told him anything like this. He thought Spinney was kidding him.

"No tackle should try to overpower a guard," Spinney went on. "It's impossible. Why don't you . . ."

As Spinney suggested several moves, Jordan listened carefully. What the Colt guard said made sense.

Jordan thanked him as they neared their respective locker rooms. "I'll work on those moves," he promised.

Jordan did work hard on them, and they were successful. But he wondered what would happen when he played against Spinney again. The next time the Packers opposed the Colts, Jordan was not sure what to do. He feared that Spinney would think that he was a "fish." But he decided to use the moves.

Spinney, of course, was prepared for Jordan's tactics. He was one of the NFL's best guards at the time and handled Jordan successfully throughout the game.

"They didn't work for me that day," Jordan says, "but they did against other guards. Art Spinney did me a big favor."

Spinney, however, had not done a favor for the other NFL guards who were supposed to handle Henry Jordan. In addition to employing his defensive tactics, Jordan occasionally has talked the opposing guards into trouble. Once an opposing team needed short yardage for an important first down. As the guard crouched at the line of scrimmage, Jordan glared at him.

"You're not quick enough to get me," Henry said.

The guard jumped offside and the ensuing five-yard penalty got the Packers out of trouble. Recalling the incident before his retirement following the 1969 season, Henry laughed and rubbed his chest.

"I don't know if it was worth it," he said. "That guard knocked me ten yards."

This is a fanciful exaggeration. Nobody had ever knocked Henry Jordan ten yards.

DICK "NIGHT TRAIN" LANE
Cornerback

The Green Bay Packers were watching game films during one of their training sessions. On the movie screen Dick "Night Train" Lane, the left cornerback of the Detroit Lions, crouched as he waited for the opposing flankerback to come at him. At the snap, the flanker sped at Lane, as if about to run a deep pattern. But he suddenly veered toward the sideline for a short pass. Fooled only momentarily, Lane recovered and smashed into the pass receiver, jarring the ball loose. One of Lane's teammates pounced on the fumble.

Watching the film, Vince Lombardi, then coach of the Green Bay Packers, slammed his right hand on the table.

"Look at Lane on that one," Lombardi said. "Look at that if you want to see a cat in operation."

Lombardi called Night Train Lane "the best cornerback I've ever seen"—a high compliment. And most people in the National Football League agree.

Lane, who later worked in the Lion front office, was so good that opposing coaches usually ordered their quarterbacks *never* to throw a pass near Lane's area. As a result, a receiver was often useless when Lane covered him. To offset this, the San Francisco 49ers once altered their offensive formation specifically to avoid Lane. Instead of lining up on the right side as he usually did, receiver R. C. Owens lined up on the left side, where he would be covered by another Lion defensive back.

"People go broke throwing into Lane's zone," explained Red Hickey, who was the 49er coach at the time. "We want to keep Owens away from him."

With Lane on the other side of the field, Owens caught seven passes. The 49er receiver who had to operate in Lane's area caught only one.

Quite often Night Train Lane caught more passes than the receiver he was covering. When he retired after the 1964 season, he held the NFL record of 14 interceptions in one season. He also had intercepted more passes than any other defensive back except Emlen Tunnell. During his 13-season career, Lane picked off 68 passes, compared to Tunnell's record of 79.

Professional football teams spend hundreds of thousands of dollars each season to scout college players. But during the summer of 1952 none of them knew much about Dick Lane. He

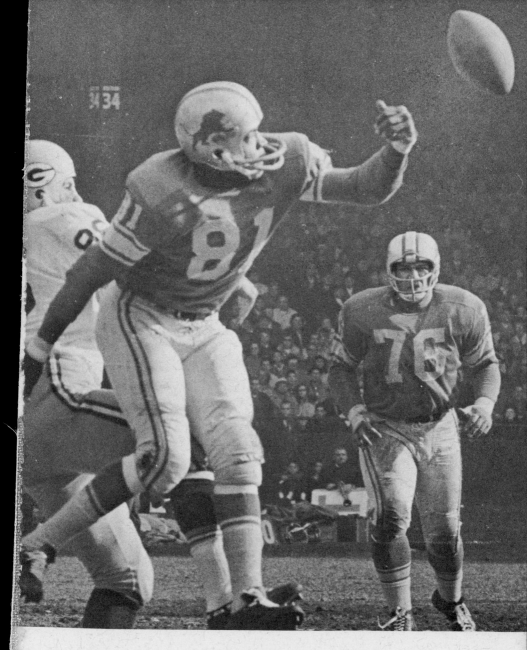

"Night Train" Lane knocks down a pass intended for Green Bay's Ron Kramer.

walked into the offices of the Los Angeles Rams
clutching an Army discharge and his college
scrapbook wrapped in brown paper. At the time,
he had been out of college for five years. He had
played offensive end for Scottsbluff (Nebraska)
Junior College in 1947 and he had received honorable mention for the Little All-America teams.
After college he spent the next three seasons in
the Army, where he played service football at
Fort Ord, California, not far from San Francisco.
The 49ers had shown some interest in him, but
not enough to offer him a contract. When he was
discharged from the Army, his wife was expect-
ing a baby and he went looking for a job.

"I got one in an aircraft factory near Los Angeles," he once said, "but it wasn't what I thought it
would be. They said I'd be a file clerk and I
thought I'd work in an office. I was a filer, all
right. I filed big sheets of metal into bins."

Oil oozed from the sheets of metal. When he
lifted them the oil dripped onto his head and all
over his clothes. "That oil ruined 15 pairs of
khakis," he said.

Eventually he became so discouraged that he
quit. The next day he was riding a bus on Bev-
erly Boulevard in Los Angeles, looking for another job, when a sign caught his eye.

LOS ANGELES RAMS, the sign said.

He got off at the next stop and walked back to
the Ram office. But he didn't go in right away.
Inside, one of the Ram secretaries noticed that a

tall man with the look of a football player was shuffling around on the sidewalk. She left her desk and walked to the doorway. Calling him over, she asked if she could help him. Lane replied that he wanted to see the Rams' coach, but couldn't remember his name. She told him that Coach Stydahar was in his office and might be able to see him.

Stydahar was conferring with two of his assistant coaches, Red Hickey and Hamp Pool. When the secretary told him about the stranger, Stydahar shrugged and said, "Show him in."

Entering the office, Lane mumbled nervously, "My name is Dick Lane, sir. I've played a little football and I'd like to have a chance to make your team."

"Where did you play?" Stydahar asked.

"Scottsbluff Junior College in Nebraska. I made Little All-America there as an end. I played Army ball at Ford Ord. The 49ers told me I was pretty good."

"Then why didn't they sign you?"

"I don't know," Lane said. "They just didn't."

"How much do you weigh?" Red Hickey asked.

"One-eighty-five," the slim-hipped Lane said, padding his weight by a few pounds.

"Where are you hiding it?" asked Hickey, who was quite used to estimating an athlete's weight.

Lane smiled sheepishly. But Stydahar had already sized him up. "All right," the head coach said, "we'll give you a look. We'll give you a contract for $4,500 for the season, but you have to make the club. It's what we call a conditional contract. We give it to all the free agents. But if you don't make the club, we don't owe you anything. Fair enough?"

"Fair enough," Lane said, signing the contract.

Recalling that day, Lane has said, "I didn't walk into the house that night, I floated." But he had misjudged the situation and had assumed that by merely showing up at the training camp he would make the team. He told some of his neighbors that he was going to play for the Rams. They sneered.

"You?" one of them said. "You play with the Rams? Don't make me laugh."

Lane vowed he would show them they were wrong. But during his first few days at camp, he began to doubt himself. At the training camp Lane was so nervous that he didn't eat for three days and fainted on the first day of practice. He was assigned to play offensive end, but he had a great deal of trouble understanding the intricate pass patterns used in pro football. At Scottsbluff he had simply outrun the defensive backs. Now he had to outmaneuver them. In addition, he had to be at an exact spot at an exact moment. Lane kept making mistakes.

"If you don't learn these plays," Red Hickey told him one day, "you better pack your things and go home."

Desperate, Lane studied his playbook hour after hour. He even purchased a small flashlight and after "lights out" at 11:00 P.M., he huddled under the covers and studied his playbook some more. He also talked with Tom Fears, then a spectacular pass receiver for the Rams. Every day after practice Lane would go to Fears's room to talk about pass patterns. And, this, strangely, is how he got his nickname.

Fears had a record player in his room and one of his favorite recordings was called "Night Train." By coincidence, "Night Train" always seemed to be playing in the background when Lane was chatting with Fears. One day Ben Sheets, who was Fears's roommate, walked into the room. Day after day, Sheets had seen Lane sitting there while "Night Train" was coming out of the record player.

"Well," Sheets said this time, "here's Night Train visiting us again."

Other players heard it and the nickname stuck. At first Lane didn't like it. But soon he came to enjoy it. After that most people never learned his correct first name. They knew him only as Night Train Lane. Later on, to players around the NFL, he was known as "Train."

But in those early days with the Rams, he was a nobody. Soon the coaches gave up on him as an offensive end. They decided to try him at defensive end, still without success. Then one day, during a scrimmage, Coach Stydahar told

Lane to move over to the cornerback position.

On his first play, Dan Towler, the Ram full-back, swept around end. As Lane moved up, one of Towler's blockers bumped him. Lane lost his balance and did a somersault in mid-air.

Somehow he landed on both feet and, quite accidentally, crashed into Towler. The big full-back went sprawling. Nearby, Stydahar smiled and shouted at Lane from the sideline.

"Great play, kid," the coach yelled. "Great play."

Turning to one of his aides, Stydahar said, "Maybe we found the kid's position."

Indeed they had. As a rookie, Lane set his NFL record of 14 interceptions during one season.

Richard Lane was born on April 16, 1928, in Austin, Texas. He was raised by his foster mother, who feared he was too small to play football. At the time he was the smallest boy in the neighborhood.

"Give up football, Richard," she said to him one day, "and I'll buy you a saxophone or a trumpet, anything you want."

But Richard Lane wanted only to play football. As the years passed, he grew taller and stronger and became a football star at Anderson High School in Austin. Then he went on to Scotts-bluff Junior College and eventually to the Rams.

But after two seasons in Los Angeles, he was traded to the Chicago Cardinals. In 1960 he was

After breaking through blockers, Lane swoops in to grab Packer halfback Paul Hornung.

traded to the Lions, where he had some of his best seasons. At the time the Lions had many of the best defensive players in the NFL—middle linebacker Joe Schmidt, tackle Alex Karras, safetyman Yale Lary. Lane fit into their hard-nosed style of playing.

"My object," he once said, "is to stop the guy with the ball before he gains another inch."

As a cornerback, playing out wide on the flank, Lane's existence was a lonely one. He had to be prepared to be all things on all plays. He needed great speed and agility to stay with halfbacks like Lenny Moore of the Baltimore Colts and Jon Arnett of the Chicago Bears, both masters of the intricate, modern-day pass patterns. He also needed the courage and strength to enable him to stop driving fullbacks like Jimmy Brown of the Cleveland Browns and Jim Taylor of the Green Bay Packers.

Lane never was happier than when he was covering a pass receiver. "Watch the belt buckle, the waistline," he once said. "That is my secret for my position. That belt buckle is always fixed, no matter how much sashaying and faking is going on with his feet and his hands. Never look at a receiver's eyes. They'll fake you into the stands if you do. Just watch the belt buckle. His legs aren't going to go any place without that belt buckle."

Lane also felt that, when he settled into his crouch at the cornerback slot, his initial position was very important. "You must be in the proper position at all times, with the precise angle on your opponent," he said.

"The angle means that you're able to see both the passer and the receiver. Except when our linebackers blitz. You can't look at the quarterback then. He's got to get rid of the ball too fast. Another big thing is being able to recover. Once in a while a receiver has *got* to beat you. But you've got to recover. You can't ever give up. Remember, never give up."

This philosophy lay behind Lane's competitiveness throughout his whole football career. A striking example of his determination and spirit occurred in the Pro-Bowl game on January 14, 1962, at the Los Angeles Coliseum. Several days before the game he began to suffer from pains in his abdomen and felt extremely weak. He feared he had appendicitis, but, foolishly, he did not consult a doctor. The day before the game the pain worsened. Nothing he ate stayed in his stomach. After drinking two cups of tea he went to bed, but he tossed and turned all night. In the morning, after another cup of tea, Lane dressed and got into the team bus for the trip to the Los Angeles Coliseum. By the time he arrived in the Western Conference All-Stars' dressing room, he was worried enough to consult the team physician.

"Doc," he said, "I'm not feeling too good. Maybe you can give me some pills to settle my stomach."

At the goal line, Dick Lane leaps high to bat down a pass intended for Jimmy Orr of the Baltimore Colts. With only 11 seconds remaining in the game, it proved to be the play that brought the Lions a 21–14 victory.

The pills helped. "They sort of eased the pain," Lane said several days later. "I could tackle guys without feeling too much pain, but I couldn't shake the weak feeling. I've never felt so weak in my life." But as weak as he was, Lane was in the starting lineup.

Early in the game he was crouching across from Tommy McDonald, the flankerback for the Eastern Conference All Stars. Not far away, Y. A. Tittle was barking signals for the East.

"I heard Tittle holler an unusual number and I figured it may have been an audible," Lane later said, referring to a change of play at the line of scrimmage. "I was playing on top of McDonald, but I let him go the second that Tittle put the ball in the air."

Lane intercepted the pass and ran 42 yards for the West's first touchdown. His play sparked a 31-30 victory. When the game ended, he confessed to the team physician about his abdominal pains. Two days later Night Train underwent an appendectomy. "There is," he joked in the hospital, "nothing like making a few rough tackles to relax you before an appendix operation."

DICK BUTKUS
Linebacker

Rumbling through the streets of Chicago, the big bus was carrying the Baltimore Colts to O'Hare Airport after a bruising 1965 game with the Bears at Wrigley Field. Suddenly, the bus skidded to a quick stop for a red light. Behind it, an auto, unable to halt in time, thumped into the rear bumper of the bus. The vibration jolted the Colt players.

"There's Butkus again," one of them said.

His teammates laughed at the quip. But the Colts were laughing out of respect for the brawny middle linebacker of the Bears. Dick Butkus, who stands 6 feet 3 inches and weighs 245 pounds, had battered the Colt runners and blitzed the Colt passer. At the time Butkus was a rookie, but already he had earned a reputation as a demon on defense.

Even his coach, George Halas, said: "Dick Butkus is one of the greatest defensive players in the history of the Bears."

For Halas, that was quite a statement. The history of the Bears represents the history of Halas. He put the team together in Decatur, Illinois, around the time of World War I. Then he moved it to Chicago, where the Bears gained a reputation as a team of rough, tough players. Halas seems to make a special effort to get rugged players. And when other teams play the Bears, they know they're in for a battle. Butkus carries on the Bears' tradition of ruggedness, to the dismay of opponents, but to the delight of Halas.

One of Halas' favorite Bears was Clyde "Bulldog" Turner. At his peak in the 1940s, when the Bears won four NFL championships, Turner performed on both the offensive and defensive units. He was a center and a linebacker.

"But Dick Butkus," Halas has said, "is the best lineman the Bears have had since Bulldog."

Entering the 1971 season, Butkus had been selected to the All-NFL teams in five of his six seasons. Against the Green Bay Packers, Butkus once outgrappled two blockers and lunged desperately at fullback Jim Taylor. Ordinarily a cement wall would not be enough to stop Taylor. Two and three tacklers sometimes fail to bring him down. But Butkus thrust one of his huge hands at Taylor, collared the fullback and tossed him onto the turf.

"Look at that," Halas shouted happily on the

Butkus stops Green Bay's driving fullback, Jim Taylor.

sideline. "Look at the way that boy tackled Taylor."

To Butkus, tackling was a science. "When I'm the key tackler," he has said, "I won't go for the ball. In other words, if I'm all by myself, I just want to bring the man down. But if he is coming through the middle of the line and he's already been hit by two or three other guys, I go for the ball. I want to strip him down and make him drop the ball. If I can cause a fumble, that takes the heart out of the other team."

Perhaps his most important asset, though, was his determination to succeed, a necessary ingredient for any occupation. One of his teammates at the University of Illinois, tackle Gary Eickman, once commented on Butkus' dedication.

"I've known a lot of guys who talk themselves out of playing varsity ball by thinking they haven't got the talent," Eickman said, "but they're making a mistake. Kids see Dick on television and they think, 'Would I love to have the gifts he has.' But the truth is that, except for his size, Dick never had a special gift—except desire. And any kid can obtain desire. It's just a matter of wanting to work hard."

It almost seems as if Richard John Butkus was destined at birth to play for the Bears. Born on the South Side of Chicago on December 9, 1942, he grew up in an immigrant Lithuanian family of nine children, including four older brothers. Two of his brothers are even bigger than he is: Don is 6 feet 6 inches tall and weighs 200 pounds; Ron is 6 feet 4 inches tall and weighs 275 pounds. Dick's other two brothers are nearly as large: John is 6 feet 3 inches and weighs 200 pounds; Dave is 6 feet 2 inches and weighs 225 pounds.

"For a long time," Dick says with a smile, "my brothers used to surround me like trees. And two of them still do."

His brother Ron had a brief trial with the Chicago Cardinals before the franchise was transferred to St. Louis. Unfortunately, injuries hastened the end of his football career. But Ron's brief performance inspired Dick more than that of any other player.

"I just followed Ron and tried to do everything that he did right. The things he did wrong, I tried to learn from. It worked out pretty well."

Although Dick occasionally went to see the Cardinals and the Bears play in Chicago, he was a restless spectator. He had difficulty just sitting in the grandstand while others were actually playing.

"I couldn't be a spectator," he has said. "I had to be a player. I had to be closer to the action than a seat."

At the time he was attending Chicago Vocational High School, where he earned All-America schoolboy honors as a fullback. But his heart was on defense. He made 70 per cent of his team's tackles. Soon the college scouts were swamping him with offers. He could have had his pick of any Big Ten school, Notre Dame and many others. He finally selected the University of Illinois.

As early as his sophomore year, Butkus was being scouted by the pro teams. He was also impressing his teammates and the All-America selectors.

"I like the publicity," he said during his senior season at Illinois, "but this is a team game and I try not to forget the players who help me look good. When one of our defensive tackles pulls and enables me to get to the opposing quarterback and toss him for a big loss, I don't forget the player who made me look good. He was helping the team."

Because of his attitude, as well as his ability, the pro teams were eager to draft him after he was graduated in 1964. It was rumored that the Packers had made a trade with Philadelphia for the Eagles' Number One choice in the NFL draft.

According to the rules under which college players are selected, the pro team with the league's poorest won-lost record for the previous season is permitted to make the first draft choice. Vince Lombardi, the Packer coach, had anticipated that the Eagles would finish much lower than the Packers in 1964. If the Eagles did have a poor year they would have an opportunity to select Butkus at the beginning of the first round. The Eagles had a better season than expected, however, and lost their early draft choice. The Bears, who finished lower than the Eagles, therefore had a chance to draft Butkus before the Packers.

At the same time, the Denver Broncos of the AFL also selected Butkus in their draft. (In 1964 there was no common draft between the two leagues, as there is now.)

"It didn't make much difference," Butkus says. "I knew I *wanted* to play for the Bears no matter what AFL team drafted me."

The Bears had to meet his price, though. Represented by a Chicago attorney, Arthur Morse, Butkus commanded a reported sum of $200,000 in salary and bonus, a record at the time for a defensive player. Up to that time, the passers and the ball carriers had collected the big bonuses.

"We gave Butkus more money," says George Halas, "than we used to pay the entire team a few years ago."

But the money did not spoil Butkus. In order to be properly prepared for the Bear training camp, he worked out with the Illinois squad at its spring drills. One day, after a grueling session, one of the coaches blew his whistle.

"All right," the coach shouted to the players, "all seniors are excused from the rest of practice."

Butkus, however, continued to do a series of calisthenics. Finally a bystander spoke to the toiling Butkus.

"Hey, Dick," he said, "didn't you hear the coach? All the seniors have been excused."

"I'm not a senior any more," Butkus replied, grinning. "I'm a freshman—a freshman pro."

His arrival at the Bear camp for the 1965 season was delayed by a commitment to the College All-Star squad. At the All-Star camp, he was one of the most dedicated performers. One day he was practicing defensive tactics with two other linebackers, Marty Schottenheimer of the University of Pittsburgh and Don Croftscheck of Indiana University. Suddenly Schottenheimer was on his knees.

"One of my contact lenses fell out," he explained.

Butkus and several other players helped him search the grass. Soon the lens was found. Cupping it carefully between his palms, Schottenheimer strolled toward the locker room. Butkus watched him leave.

"Hey," Dick yelled, "where are you going? Let's have some more hitting."

Butkus thrives on physical contact, as he showed in the All-Star Game against the NFL champions, the Cleveland Browns. Several times

*Charging through a hole in the Giant line, Butkus
goes for the quarterback.*

he stopped Jim Brown, then the most famous fullback in football. After the game Butkus went out of his way to shake hands with Brown, a rare display of confidence for a player who had yet to earn his place with the Bears. But Jim Brown knew that Butkus would make good.

"Butkus is everything I've heard he is, strong and fast," Brown said later. "I'm glad the game is over."

For Butkus, his career was just beginning. When he reported to the Bear camp, the veterans greeted him with verbal needles. They teased him about his shoe size, a huge 11½ triple E. He was nicknamed "Paddles." They also gave investment advice for his bonus money. But Butkus smiled silently.

"The worst thing I could've done was talk back," he says. "There's no better way to make a fool of yourself than telling everyone you're going to make it big. If you can't play, they'll cut you. If you can, they'll make it their business to get to know you."

Soon the Bear veterans accepted him. His spirit had won them over.

"Well," an assistant coach said, "we've got another member of the 110% Club."

In practice, Butkus was learning the intricate assignments that baffle some rookies. He had to know the difference between the "stunts," the "revolves," the "storm," the "bullets." In addition, each of the formations in which he would blitz the quarterback had a different name— Pink, Green, Blue, Purple, Turkey, Tweedy, Pelican, and his favorite, the Mad Dog.

"In the Mad Dog," Butkus likes to say, "*everybody* goes after the quarterback."

In the season opener against the San Francisco 49ers, he made 11 unassisted tackles, a remarkable number for a rookie. But he had his problems. Bruce Bosley, the veteran center of the 49ers, cut him down a few times with good blocks. Several weeks later, in the rematch between the Bears and the 49ers, Bosley never succeeded in blocking Butkus out of the play.

"Every time I was supposed to block him," Bosley said, "he was going somewhere else. He sure improved fast."

By that time Butkus had impressed the Baltimore Colts, too. Jim Parker, the big guard, called him "the best rookie I've seen in my time in the league." Lenny Moore, the Colt halfback, commented that "Every time I made my break and saw daylight, that number 51 would be closing off the hole."

Since Butkus was not exceptionally fast, the Bears had feared that his pass coverage might suffer.

Instead, he had intercepted 15 passes through the 1970 season, a remarkable total for a middle linebacker. As a rookie, he even intercepted more

Dick Butkus intercepts a pass intended for Bill Gambrell (3) in the final quarter of a 1965 game with the Cardinals.

passes than the Bears' defensive backs. One of his most important interceptions occurred in a 1965 game against the Minnesota Vikings.

The Bears were trying to hold a 38-37 lead as the Vikings, with Fran Tarkenton at quarterback, were moving downfield. Intercepting a Tarkenton pass at the Viking 45-yard line, Butkus chugged to the 10-yard line. On the first play, Gale Sayers hurried into the end zone for the clinching touchdown.

Sayers scored 22 touchdowns that season, a league record, and an incredible accomplishment for a rookie. Had it not been for Sayers, Butkus presumably would have been selected as the NFL Rookie of the Year. George Halas had campaigned for dual rookie awards, one for offense, one for defense. But only one award was presented—to Sayers.

"That's all right," Butkus said, "as long as somebody on the Bears gets it."

Awards have never impressed Butkus too much. At Illinois, he was selected for the Athlete of the Year Award. When informed of the honor, he asked, quite innocently, "What is it?" But the honor he treasures most is the game ball he received after the Bears defeated the Detroit Lions during his rookie season.

"That ball really means something to me," he says, "because it's from my teammates."

In 1966 the Bears dropped from third place to

fifth, but Dick Butkus continued to improve. After a late-season game against the Colts, Abe Gibron, a Bear assistant coach, spoke of Butkus' performance as a second-year man.

"He's not getting the publicity he got as a rookie," Gibron said, "but he's a better player."

As proof, Butkus was again named to the Western Division All-Star team for the annual Pro-Bowl game. Only a handful of players have been selected for this honor in both of their first two seasons.

"And looking to the future," says George Halas, "I can't imagine a Pro-Bowl game without Dick Butkus in it."

Through the 1970 season, he had been selected to the Pro Bowl squad in each of his six seasons. Beyond that, he had developed into the epitome of a middle linebacker. But his reputation as a "mean" player disturbed him.

"I don't think I'm any meaner than anybody else," he said. "I just play the game the way it's supposed to be played."

About the Author

Dave Anderson has covered professional football
for many years as a sports writer for the New York
Times and earlier for the New York *Journal-
American*. He has written for the *Saturday Evening Post, True, Sports Illustrated* and *Sport* Magazine. He is the author of *Countdown to Super
Bowl* (Random House), the saga of the New York
Jets' historic upset of the Baltimore Colts in 1969,
and received the 1965 E. P. Dutton Award for Best
Sports Stories. He is also the author of *Great Quarterbacks of the NFL* and *Great Pass Receivers of
the NFL* (Punt, Pass & Kick Library #2 and #6).

Index

Page numbers in italics refer to photographs